Fantastic Cinema in the Years Before CGI

A Field Guide to Science Fiction, Horror, and Fantasy Films of the Twentieth Century

By Pierre V. Comtois

Copyrights
All Illustrations Respective Copyright Holders

Cover: FX engineers work on the set of *When Worlds Collide*. Image respective copyright holder.

Dedication
Kenneth Tobey, Grant Williams, Richard Carlson, Hugh Marlowe, Faith Domergue, Russell Johnson, Rex Reason, Val Lewton, Roger Corman, Luana Anders, Willis O'Brien, Jack Arnold, Janet Munro, Bernard Herrmann, Fritz Lang, Ray Bradbury, Gloria Talbot, Kevin McCarthey, King Donovan, Gene Barry, Marshall Thompson, William Hopper, John Agar, Mara Corday, Richard Matheson, Simone Simon, Jacques Tourneur, Robert Wise, Charlton Heston, Ray Harryhausen, James Franciscus, Michael Crichton, Byron Haskin, George Pal, Richard Carlson, Brian Donlevy, Barbara Rush, Jeff Morrow, Richard Denning, and all the other actors, writers, producers, and technicians that made the classic era of science fiction cinema the wonderful playground of ideas it was.

"Fantastic Cinema in the Years Before CGI," by Pierre V. Comtois. ISBN 978-1-947532-25-0.

Published 2017 by Virtualbookworm.com Publishing Inc., P.O. Box 9949, College Station, TX 77842, US. ©2017, Pierre V. Comtois. All rights reserved. No part of this publication may be reproduced, stored in a retrieval system, or transmitted in any form or by any means, electronic, mechanical, recording or otherwise, without the prior written permission of Pierre V. Comtois.

Contents

Introduction 6
The Lost World 10
Metropolis 12
Dracula 14
Frankenstein 16
King Kong 18
Things to Come 20
Cat People 22
I Walked With a Zombie 24
The Seventh Victim 26
The Leopard Man 28
Curse of the Cat People 30
The Uninvited 32
The Ghost and Mrs. Muir 34
Mighty Joe Young 36
Destination Moon 38
Rocketship XM 40
The Day the Earth Stood Still 42
The Thing (From Another World) 44
When Worlds Collide 46
War of the Worlds 48
The Beast From 20,000 Fathoms 50
It Came From Outer Space 52
The Magnetic Monster 54
The Twonky 56
Project Moonbase 58
Invaders From Mars 60
Them! 62
This Island Earth 64
Creature From the Black Lagoon 66
Target Earth 68
Cult of the Cobra 70
Tarantula 72
It Came From Beneath the Sea 74
Revenge of the Creature 76
The Atomic Man 78
Conquest of Space 80
Forbidden Planet 82
Invasion of the Body Snatchers 84
Earth vs the Flying Saucers 86
The Creature Walks Among Us 88
The Deadly Mantis 90
The Black Scorpion 92
The Incredible Shrinking Man 94
The Monolith Monsters 96

Title	Page
Kronos	98
20 Million Miles to Earth	100
The Quatermass Xperiment	102
Quatermass II	104
The Monster That Challenged the World	106
Attack of the Crab Monsters	108
The Fly	110
Curse of the Demon	112
It! The Thing From Beyond Space	114
Fiend Without a Face	116
I Married a Monster From Outer Space	118
The Space Children	120
The Crawling Eye	122
First Man Into Space	124
Journey to the Center of the Earth	126
Return of the Fly	128
The Time Machine	130
Village of the Damned	132
House of Usher	134
Day the Earth Caught Fire	136
Voyage to the Bottom of the Sea	138
The Innocents	140
The Pit and the Pendulum	142
Mysterious Island	144
Burn, Witch, Burn!	146
Panic in Year Zero	148
Carnival of Souls	150
Jason and the Argonauts	152
Day of the Triffids	154
The Haunted Palace	156
The Haunting	158
First Men in the Moon	160
Masque of the Red Death	162
Robinson Crusoe on Mars	164
The Time Travelers	166
The Last Man on Earth	168
Children of the Damned	170
Tomb of Ligeia	172
Planet of the Vampires	174
Die, Monster, Die!	176
Curse of the Fly	178
Incubus	180
Fantastic Voyage	182
One Million Years B.C.	184
Fahrenheit 451	186
Seconds	188
2001: A Space Odyssey	190
The Planet of the Apes	192

The Power	194
Five Million Miles to Earth	196
Valley of the Gwangi	198
When Dinosaurs Ruled the Earth	200
The Dunwich Horror	202
Colossus: The Forbin Project	204
Beneath the Planet of the Apes	206
THX 1138	208
The Andromeda Strain	210
Duel	212
The Omega Man	214
The Night Stalker	216
Soylent Green	218
The Legend of Hell House	220
The Night Strangler	222
Phase IV	224
The Terminal Man	226
The Stepford Wives	228
Rollerball	230
Trilogy of Terror	232
The Land That Time Forgot, People That Time Forgot, At the Earth's Core	234
Logan's Run	236
Star Wars, Empire Strikes Back, Return of the Jedi	238
Invasion of the Body Snatchers (1978)	240
Coma	242
Star Trek: The Motion Picture, Wrath of Khan, Search for Spock, Voyage Home, Final Frontier, Undiscovered Country	244
Alien	246
Altered States	248
Excalibur	250
Outland	252
Bladerunner	254
Something Wicked This Way Comes	256
Dune, Frank Herbert's Dune, Children of Dune	258

Introduction

I've been in love with the fantastic and fantastic movies for as long as I can remember. Which one I was exposed to first, whether literary or cinematic, is more difficult to sort out but whichever it was, the vistas of the future, the possibilities of science, the limitlessness of the imagination represented in either science fiction or fantasy, grabbed me from the very first.

Alongside early readings of Tom Swift, there was *Fantasmic Features* on Saturday afternoons where I first encountered Kenneth Tobey and Grant Williams as they met the challenge of alien invaders, giant monsters, and science run amok in films produced through the 1950s and not much later, at my local theater where low budget fare such as *Planet of the Vampires* rubbed shoulders with horror and the supernatural. Later in the 1960s, as I graduated from the Strand to suburban cineplexes, cinematic fantasy and SF grew up with me as supernatural evil was left behind for such up to date threats as deadly microbes from space, renegade computers, and dystopian futures.

Then came the great dividing line, the film that ended the reign of classic SF themes and tropes of the 1950s and 60s and, merging science fiction and fantasy, launched the modern era of SF cinema dominated by guns and action rather than people and ideas. That film was *Star Wars*.

Star Wars harkened back to the more simplistic, pre atom age era of the cliff hanger serials of the 1940s. Governed by fast moving plots and furious action, the old time serials were designed to enthrall kids and keep them coming back to the theater every week. Any more serious content made it into the films by accident. Such were the antecedents of *Star Wars* which brought the cliff hanger tropes up to date with amazing special effects and engaging, albeit stereotypical, characters.

The combination proved potent as the movie not only attracted the notice of SF film fans, but drew in a wider audience that never before considered the science fiction or fantasy genres as anything but kid stuff. The wild success of *Star Wars* proved to be a double edged sword for more serious minded fantasy fans in general and science fiction fans in particular. On the one hand, it created a boom in the cinema of the fantastic with every Hollywood studio suddenly investing serious money in science fiction/fantasy films but on the other, made empty headed "big gun action" and elaborate FX (made worse with the arrival of CGI) the prime attractions for thrill hungry audiences whose tastes had now been irrevocably fashioned by George Lucas.

But the advent of *Star Wars* has not wiped out all memory of what came before. The high frontiers explored by the great SF/fantasy films of the 1950s and 60s still exist. Their promise of shining futures and threats to the human spirit are still relevant today, perhaps all the more so in a cinematic environment governed by secular humanism, political correctness, and mindless action. Their ideas and themes and values are what qualify these films as "classics" referring back to a time from which somehow, the world took a wrong turn, and pointing to futures that might have been and could yet be if society would only come to its senses.

Thus, the following book, which began life at the turn of the new century when the current craze was for drawing up "100 best of" lists, whether the greatest thinkers of all time, the greatest novels of all time, the most important women of all time, or the greatest films of all time. Most of these lists lacked legitimacy due to their obvious deference to political correctness, that is, certain entries had to be included in the name of fairness even if there might have been many others more deserving. For instance, a 100 best films list was more or less broken down by decade so that no age group would feel left out. Now let's face it, if a real list of the 100 best films of all time were compiled there probably wouldn't be many movies on it made after 1960. Instead, there was the spectacle of films such as *Fargo,* which had only been released in 1996 on the twentieth century's 100 best list! Now how can any serious judgment of such a new film have been made against say, 50 years of critical analysis of other films? Answer: there couldn't have been.

And so, where does all that leave SF/fantasy movie fans? Where's the definitive guide to help them navigate the ocean of product that Hollywood has pumped out over the past few decades? Well, it leaves them with this current volume which began life as a list of the top 100 SF films of all time before morphing into simply a combination of the best or most interesting or just plain fun SF/fantasy/horror films of all time.

In deciding which films deserve to be included in this compendium, there will be no concessions to the reader's age, gender, or political persuasion. The only elements that will be considered are (in descending order of importance): the film's entertainment value and how wide an audience it succeeded in reaching; what ideas and themes did the film explore; the complexity and multi-textuality of the film's plot; and the film's technical, directorial, and cinematographic achievement.

With those points in mind, the films listed in this volume ended up falling roughly between the years 1950-1975 with occasional forays backward and forward in time. Based on the above criteria, the best films were those that preserved or captured the values of post war America and the West in general, portrayal of the scientist hero (as opposed to the mad scientist of pre-World War II years), and respect for the military. Together, these elements gave the best films, no matter how outlandish the setting or situation, a grounding in reality, something modern films with all their advanced production values, often lack.

This foundation might be defined as the values of the "greatest generation." The values that brought America's civilization to its zenith in the 1950s; encompassing the hard learned lessons of sacrifice and duty from the Depression and world war. Part of the success of that American civilization reflected in most of these films, was the fact that the nation had not yet moved into a post-Christian world, perhaps explaining why the best SF movies were about hope, something also lacking in modern films which all too often end in darkness and pointless materialism leaving viewers wondering what all the fuss was about.

Of course there were plenty of bad movies in the 1950-75 period, but the reasons for their falling short was due mainly to inept storytelling, failure to take their subject matter seriously by the producers, or they simply had no redeeming value. Although later films are uniformly well produced, most fail as good movies not just due to story or bad FX, but mainly because of their assault on the sensibilities of the audiences liberally laced as they are by foul language and questionable ethics that vitiate whatever positive qualities they might have.

Finally, one caveat: personal idiosyncracies. Despite the bold list of criteria outlined above, I admit that it was impossible to be completely objective in judging these films. Nevertheless, I feel confident that the listing here is more than defensible. I tried to list them from best to least best, then to categorize them by genre, then group them into honorable mentions, also rans, or extra credits but all proved inadequate. I finally gave up as they all had at least something to recommend them. Finally, I settled for the tried and true chronological order and to leave it to the reader to seek out the films and judge for themselves the accuracy of my comments. One hint: the best films will emphasize the light and dark sides of man. They might be idea driven or emphasize man's idealism or his most primal fears (even as man enters his third millennium or moves out on new voyages of discovery, he takes along all his old fears and paranoias). Lesser films that don't succeed in reaching those rarefied heights might still be idea driven or have a psychological edge. But serious or not, every film here will have its quota of entertainment value. In fact, some might simply be classified as just plain fun!

One other thing. "Adult" elements began to make their presence felt in many post 1970 films. And though I've deliberately left out any film that crossed a line from family friendly to adults only, there are some that, while good, idea driven films, do contain mature content of a limited nature which I've duly labeled.

So enjoy this light hearted tour of the best of SF/fantasy cinema. One in which I've tried to keep my "capsule reviews" brief if not succinct so as not to overwhelm the reader with boring analysis. (Although my enthusiasm for particular films might get the best of me at times!) Accompanied by select illustrations, I hope the format will prove less harmless than entertaining.

Pierre V. Comtois
October 2017

The Lost World (1925)

Don't let the film's lack of sound (or color for that matter) keep you from enjoying the heck out of this early cinema classic! Although primitive by later standards, *The Lost World* established a number of precedents that would become standard for the genre in later years. Arthur Conan Doyle's plot of a scientific expedition up the Amazon River to seek a remote plateau where dinosaurs still roam became a staple of giant monster films (creature is freed or captured and ends up rampaging through famous cities). No less influential than Doyle's story was the amazing special FX of stop motion master Willis O'Brien, whose skill at compositing his models into scenes with live actors stunned audiences at the time and to some degree, still does! (The technique was still being used in the early 1970s!) And if all those dinosaur action scenes aren't enough, then check out this film's final contribution to the genre: the romantic co-star! That tradition started off with a bang here with cute Bessie Love (nee Juanita Horton). Who's she? Who cares? She may be a forgotten actress of the silent era, but her addition to *The Lost World* while obviously set decoration, nevertheless became an integral part for practically every fantasy film to follow. Female co-stars, be they fellow scientists or gal Fridays, gave all the fantastic goings on a human dimension and grounded them in a reality that they might have lost amid the action and FX. Fer sher, with *The Lost World*, the cinema of the fantastic was off to a strong start!

The magic of Willis O'Brien! Members of Prof. Challenger's expedition are cornered by a pair of stop motion dinosaurs.

Bessie Love dons the jodhpurs for her role in *The Lost World*.

Willis O'Brien hard at work in his studio animating a dinosaur sequence for *The Lost World*.

Our cast: Lloyd Hughes as Ed Malone, Walter Beery as Prof. Challenger, and Bessie Love as Paula White.

Metropolis (1927)

For a silent classic whose message spoke more strongly before the collapse of the Berlin Wall, this film still provides the viewer with powerful ideas regarding the relationship between labor and capital. Perhaps in a world of increasing electronic complexity and instantaneous communications where the individual worker becomes less and less a factor in business decisions, what this film has to say may continue to be relevant beyond its simplistic Marxian origins. That said, it's safe to say that *Metropolis* is director Fritz Lang's masterpiece. Aided and abetted by wife Thea von Harbou who wrote the script, it tells the tale of Freder, the son of a rich one percenter who, wanting to find out what life is like for the lower classes, travels to the city's lowest levels and finds out. There, he falls in love with working girl Maria. Meanwhile, mad scientist and some time sorcerer, Rotwang, builds a robot duplicate of the girl and uses it to seduce debauched one percenter aristocracy while at the same time undermining Maria's attempts at peaceful coexistence between the upper and lower classes. Luckily there's a happy ending but not before we get spectacular scenes of the futuristic Metropolis and monster machines tended by thousands of worker drones! It was all thanks to early FX master Eugen Schufftan. The discerning fantasy fan will also appreciate Rotwang's gothic HQ, the modernistic upper levels of the city, and the creation of the robot Maria accompanied by impressive electrical effects. Recent discoveries of missing portions of the film have resulted in a restored version that's rather longish but still satisfying with plenty of symbolic sub-text that leaves viewers thinking. A monumental achievement in the cinema of the fantastic and the best kind of SF.

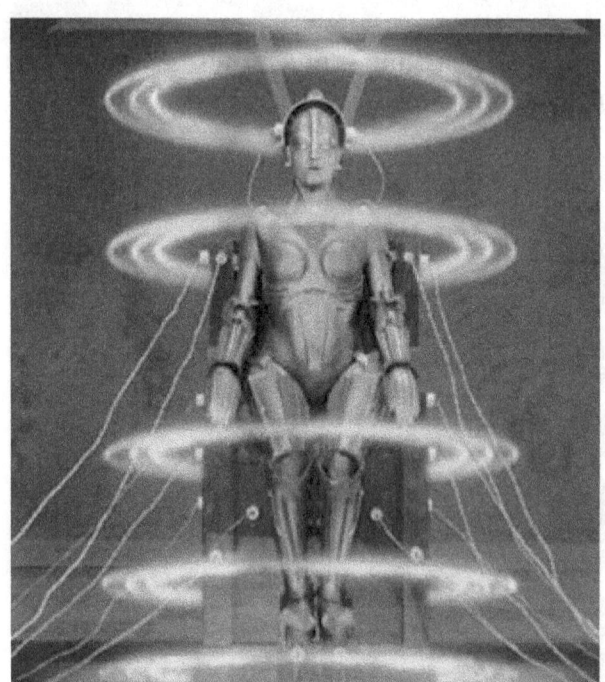

After and before: The Maria robot by Eugen Schufftan.

Brigitte Helm as Maria.

The central tower of Metropolis where Freder lived until a meeting with Maria inspired him to find out about the workers whose toil allowed him his life of ease.

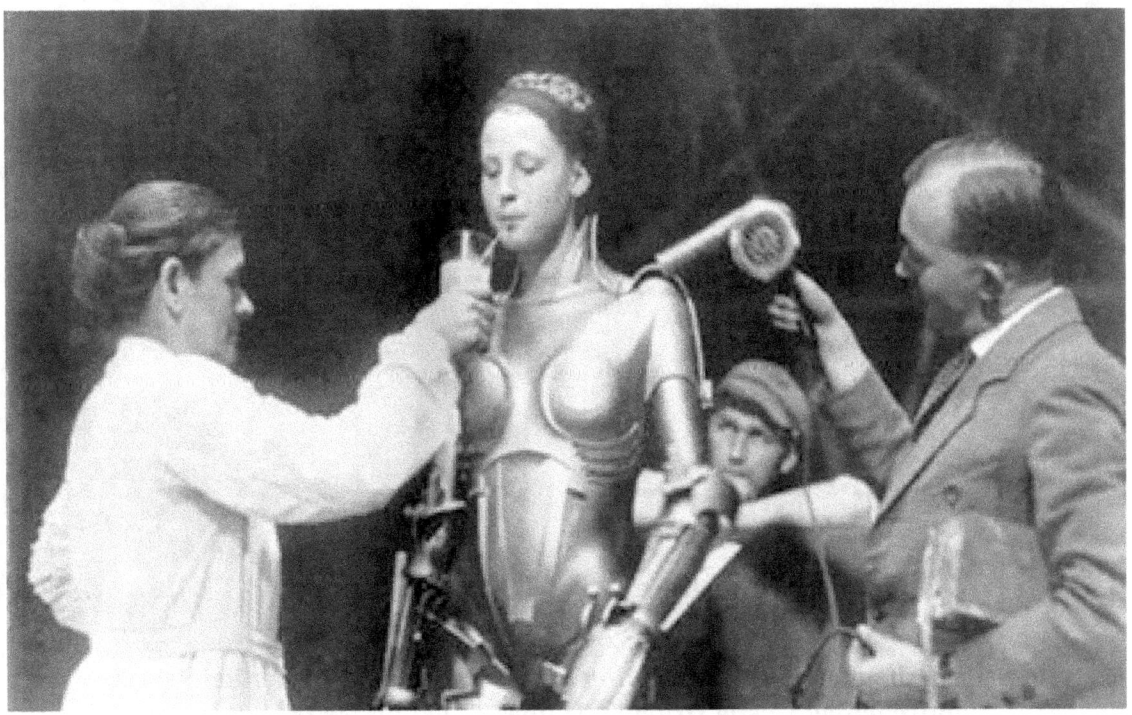
Brigitte Helm is prepped for her role as the evil robot.

Dracula (1931)

The gang's all here: Edward Van Sloan as Van Helsing, Helen Chandler as Mina Seward, and Dwight Fry as the irrepressible Renfield but somehow they don't add up to the sum of their parts. Dull direction by Todd Browning and a wooden performance by Bela Lugosi as the Count don't help either. The real star in this admittedly groundbreaking film are the sets that supply atmosphere aplenty beginning with the whole opening sequence in Transylvania. The introduction of Renfield as he rides into the village aboard a horse drawn coach and his subsequent ride through the Borgo Pass to castle Dracula is textbook for matte paintings. But it doesn't stop there! Dropped off at the pass, Renfield is met by another coach driven by Dracula himself who then whips through the gloomy countryside in a mad frenzy. Castle Dracula itself is a masterpiece of gothic mood and menace especially the interior with its rubble strewn floors and massive, cobwebbed staircase. Here, Lugosi gives his best performance in the film as his eyes express eager hunger when Renfield pricks his finger and draws a bead of blood. The whole introductory sequence is topped off in a weird scene showing Dracula rising from his coffin along with a trio of vampiric "wives" all desperate to feed on the hapless Renfield. The rest of the film is somewhat restrained after that with most of the action taking place in the neat surroundings of the Seward home until the climax at Carfax Abbey. Despite its sometimes glacial pace, the film is rightly a classic in that its success made the horror movie a cinema staple forever after.

Setting the mood: matte painting for *Dracula* showing Renfield's coach approaching Castle Dracula. It doesn't get better than this, folks!

Renfield arrives at Castle Dracula. Dig the giant spider web at the top of the stairs!

Bet you didn't know he was even married! Dracula warns off his wives from the unconscious Renfield.

Our cast reviews the plot of Dracula: Bela Lugosi, David Manners, Dwight Fry, and Edward Van Sloan look over Helen Chandler's shoulder as she reads from the original novel.

Frankenstein (1931)

"It's alive!!!" What more need be said about this classic? Well, maybe a few words more. Produced on the heels of the successful *Dracula*, Universal Studios discovered that the box office gold dug up by the earlier film was no fluke as its production of *Frankenstein* quickly demonstrated. Directed by the more versatile James Whale, the movie was considerably more fast paced than its predecessor with more animated acting from Colin Clive as Henry Frankenstein, Mae Clark as Elizabeth Lavenza, and of course, Boris Karloff as the Monster. Sure, Clive's infamous words uttered at the moment when his creature comes to life was attention grabbing (representing as it did, the mad scientist's challenge to God the Creator Himself), but it was the menacing yet sympathetic performance of Karloff as the monster that takes this film across the finish line. At once terrifying in his threats to Frankenstein and his fiancé as well as the little girl he drowns, and kindly in his relation to the blind man, Karloff managed to humanize his character allowing audiences to see past the scary makeup that covered his face and glimpse the soul beneath. Again, as in *Dracula*, atmosphere was everything with shots of Frankenstein's castle and laboratory, foggy forests of denuded trees, and the final scene at the windmill helping to provide the chills. Although fun stuff for the nostalgic, it does show its age and is still a far cry from the existentialism of Mary Shelley's original novel.

This scene in which the monster ends up drowning the little girl was removed by censors and not seen for decades. Making it all the more disturbing was Karloff's ability to demonstrate emotion even under all of his makeup. One moment he could be sympathetic and the next horrifying.

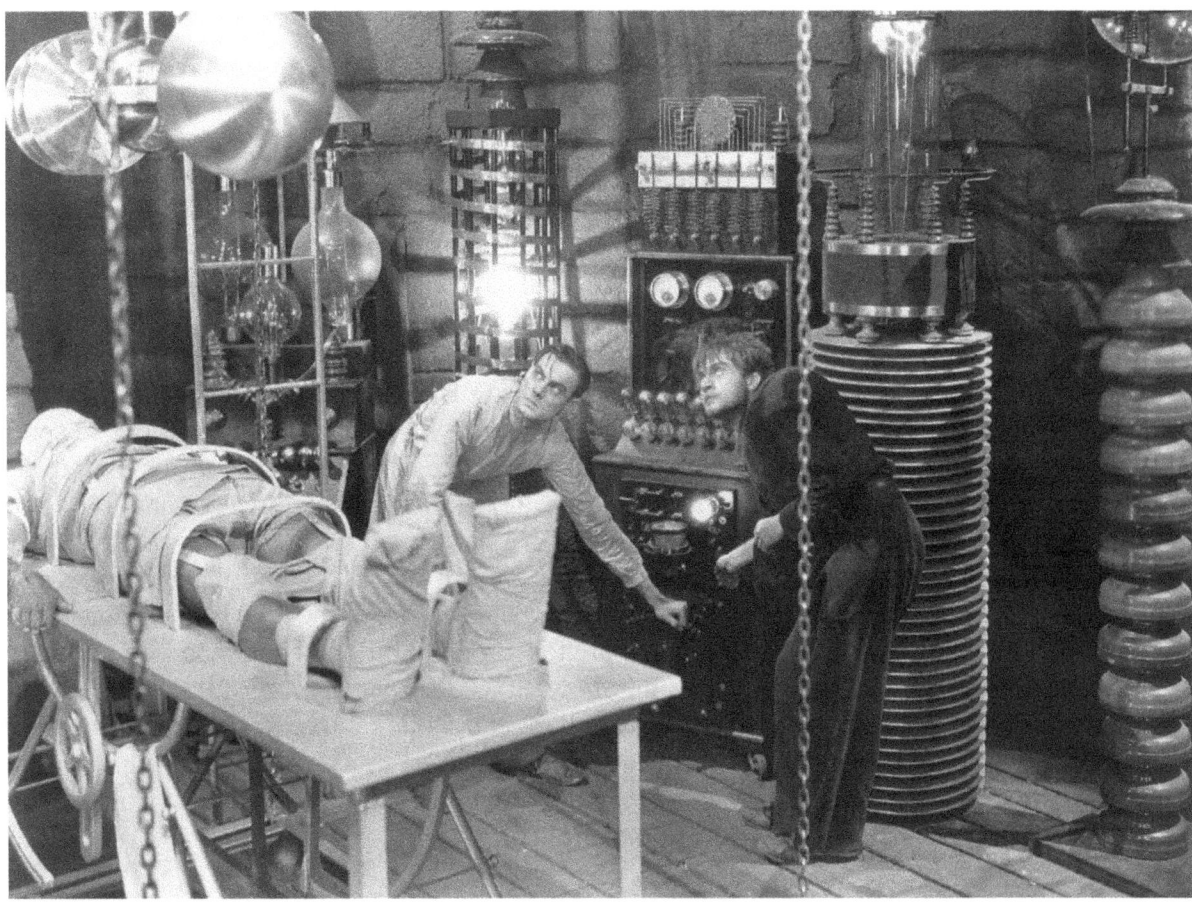

Colin Clive as Frankenstein and Dwight Fry as Fritz hold their collective breaths as the switch is thrown that will bring life to the monster. Clive's action will also stereotype scientists in fantasy films as "mad" for the next twenty years!

Frankenstein strikes at another instinctual fear as the monster comes to Elizabeth (Mae Clark) on her wedding night.

King Kong (1933)

Action, adventure, romance, and a groundbreaking combination of stop motion and matte painting FX makes this film not only an early masterpiece of the fantastic, but one that has remained timeless and vastly entertaining decade after decade. Filled with memorable scenes that have burned themselves into the American psyche including: Kong shaking his human pursuers from a giant log into a vine veiled canyon; sailors being chased and eaten across a fog bound swamp; Kong's battle with the pterodactyl; and Kong's last stand atop the Empire State Building! Once again, stop motion master Willis O'Brien does the honors and what a difference eight years made! O'Brien's models move more smoothly than ever and sport more anatomical precision as they charge through the jungle, fly through the air, or slink through swamps that are flawlessly integrated with matte paintings, miniature sets, and live actors…all at once! He even manages to imbue Kong with a human dimension that by picture's end, earns him the sympathy of viewers. Although Robert Armstrong as Carl Denham overacts and Bruce Cabot as Jack Driscoll is wooden…certainly not deserving of the love of the beautiful Faye Wray…the plot, FX, and Kong himself are too strong to be held back much. But of the human actors, Wray as Ann Darrow, steals the show. Sure, she spends most of it screaming, but who could blame Kong for his fascination with her? A fascination that winds up causing his death. Denham's final line about "It was beauty killed the beast" was more than fitting, referring as it does to how a woman could end up being the ruin of a good man! Warning: Don't be fooled by later remakes, none hold a candle to the original!

Easy to see here what Kong saw in Fay Wray!

This matte shot of the approach to Skull Island showing the wall the natives built to hold back Kong goes a long way to set the mood for the horrors to follow.

Kong battles a tyrannosaurus rex in one of Willis O'Brien's most amazing sequences. And that's a live shot of Fay Wray at bottom right.

Things to Come (1936)

H.G.Wells' vision of the near future (in this case, World War II) and then the far future is engagingly rendered onto the big screen by Wells himself (script), William Cameron Menzies (direction) and Alexander Korda (set design). With enough material for a half dozen movies (the future war, a world where civilization is thrown back to the dark ages, the secret foundation where knowledge is preserved and whose members only await the right moment to emerge and reestablish civilization, the disease that wipes out most of mankind, a future world that sets progress against modern Luddites, the test flight of the first rocket into space), this film fulfills the first requirement of all great SF: the presentation of ideas and concepts. Divided into three parts (the future war that wipes out civilization, the new dark age, and the super scientific future), Wells' central theme is the triumph of a militant secularism that pits the forces of ignorance (represented in the film by artists and social conservatives fearful of progress) against those of reason (in the form of scientists determined to push the boundaries of knowledge). The film's missionary of science is Raymond Massey as John Cabal, a member of a secret foundation called Wings Over the World (that Cabal describes variously as "the freemasons of science," "the brotherhood of efficiency," and "the government of common sense!") who arrives in the camp of "the Boss," a local warlord played by Ralph Richardson to proclaim the gospel of reason. Richardson's overthrow heralds the start of an extended FX sequence supervised by Ned Mann that's truly remarkable as the world of the future is constructed right before our eyes. However, Wells' thematic sub-text, suggesting that in order to achieve the utopia depicted in the film, man would necessarily have to divest himself of religion and other illogical belief systems, renders his wonderful future sterile and purposeless, an eventuality that Cabal, in a final, ringing speech, fails to reconcile in a convincing manner. That said, *Things To Come* remains as one of the most thought provoking achievements of fantastic cinema.

Margaretta Scott shows off the styles of 2036.

This theater poster is vaguely reminiscent of Soviet propaganda posters of the time.

John Cabal (left) informs the Boss that his days are numbered.

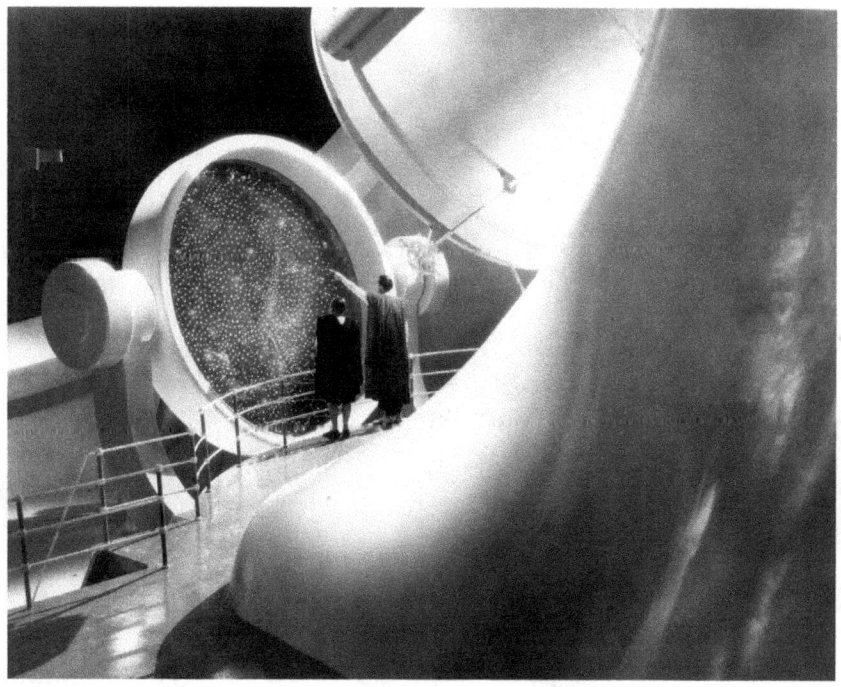

Oswald Cabal exhorts over man's destiny; but what good is it if man should gain the whole universe but lose his soul?

Cat People (1942)

Moody, evocative direction by Jacques Tourneur makes this throw away b-film memorable with sultry Simone Simon (and her wonderful accent!) caught in a story fraught with sexual tension. Producer Val Lewton embarked on a string of classy "horror" movies in the 1940s including *I Walked With a Zombie, The Seventh Victim*, and *Ghost Ship*. But where Universal Studios did it with monsters, Lewton took a more subtle approach (partially because he had less money to spend) and came away with the superior product. Of which *Cat People* is the flagship with its black and white cinematography by Nicholas Musuraca, suggestive plot, and good cast including Kent Smith as Oliver Reed, the frustrated lover and husband; Jane Randolph as Alice Moore, the co-worker who secretly pines for him; and of course, Simon as Irena Dubrovna. Our story begins innocently enough when Reed meets Irena at the zoo. After a whirlwind courtship, they marry with the understanding that the marriage cannot be consummated. Irena, you see, is fearful that if she allows her passions to run free, she'll transform into a man eating panther and kill her husband! Is her fear real or just a psychological hangup? It's never made quite clear except that certain incidents during the course of film suggest the former. Take for example, Jane Randolph's being stalked by something unseen that forces her into the basement pool of a shadowy health club. We never see her pursuer, but strange growls and animal grunts suggest it wasn't her imagination. Was it Simon in her cat persona or Randolph's imagination? You be the judge!

Simone Simon as Irena Dubrovna in *Cat People*. So what if she was a little shy about intimacy? She was definitely worth waiting for!

Jane Randolph as Alice Moore, just before jumping into the pool, wonders if those are the growls of a big cat she hears…

Irena considers telling Oliver about the legend of the cat people...

In one of the most iconic moments of *Cat People*, Jane Randolph as Alice Moore looks over her shoulder thinking she hears the sounds of pursuit...

I Walked With a Zombie (1943)

Absolutely scrumptious black and white film by director Jacques Tourneur and producer Val Lewton about a young nurse (Betsy Connell played by attractive Frances Dee) who travels to the West Indies to care for a planter's wife who has fallen into a strange lethargy. Like *Cat People*, *I Walked With a Zombie* leaves interpretation of the action up to the viewer: is it to be taken literally or pscychologically? Surely, the fact that Dr. Rand, played by Edith Barrett, turns out to be the hidden voice of Damballah or whatever during a voodoo ceremony would suggest the latter. But then, what about the zombie creature Betsy encounters amid the sugar cane which later, is seen carrying the body of Jessica Holland (played by Christine Gordon) into the sea? Regardless, cinematography by J. Roy Hunt is pure eye candy with the night scene of Betsy and Jessica moving through the field of sugar cane and coming face to face with the zombie being the epitome of atmospheric weirdness! Alone, worth the price of admission! But don't discount night scenes of darkened bedrooms, shadow haunted battlements, and moonlit beaches. All combine with a thoughtful script by Curt Siodmak to create a true horror classic!

Jessica and Betsy (Christine Gordon and Frances Dee) encounter the zombie after a spooky walk through the cane fields.

Betsy learns from Dr. Rand (right) that she has to go along with the natives' superstitions in order to get them to accept the benefits of modern medicine.

So who wouldn't want to be nursed back to health by Frances Dee?

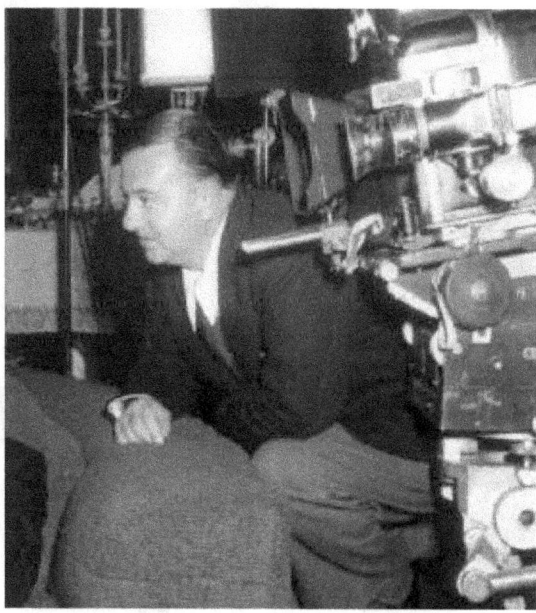

Director Jacques Tourneur, master of mood and atmosphere.

The Seventh Victim (1943)

Another Val Lewton produced instant classic this time directed by Mark Robson who manages to keep this tale about a coven of devil worshippers from veering into the realm of a Nancy Drew mystery with a series of bizarre images including an empty room furnished with nothing but a hangman's noose and chair, a subway car empty but for a pair of tuxedoed drunks hauling a corpse, and a downright weird shower scene where heroine Mary Gibson, played by Kim Hunter, is interrupted while bathing by a shadowed figure on the other side of the curtain warning her to mind her own business! Mary, you see, has come to the big city to look for her sister (played by Jean Brooks) who has disappeared. Turns out she's joined a coven and, deciding to quit, is being psychologically pressured to commit suicide. But perhaps weirdest of all is the amorous attention Mary receives from the various men in the story (including a pre-*Leave it to Beaver* Hugh Beaumont) despite the fact that she's supposed to be a schoolgirl! Near the climax of the film, Tom Conway, in the person of Dr. Louis Judd, tells off the murderous cultists making hash of their rationalizations and punctuating his argument with a recitation of the Lord's Prayer. Throughout, Robson does fellow Lewton director Jacques Tourneur proud by escorting the viewer expertly through a maze of lies, deceits, and hidden agendas all clothed in beautiful black and white cinematography by Nicholas Musuraca to the final shocking scene when Mary's sister hangs herself off screen. A forgotten gem!

The top flight cast of *The Seventh Victim* (l to r): Kim Hunter (Mary Gibson), Jean Brooks (Jacqueline Gibson), and Tom Conway (Dr. Louis Judd).

The banal face of evil: members of the coven listen as Dr. Judd (off screen) tells them off.

Mary Gibson (Kim Hunter) receives a visitor while caught in the shower!

The Leopard Man (1943)

Val Lewton and Jacques Tourneur strike again! This time focusing on a small southwestern town seemingly threatened by a loose leopard. It seems that manager/boyfriend Jerry Manning (Dennis O'Keefe) has added a leopard to Kiki Walker's (Jean Brooks) nightclub act which then escapes. The killings that follow are assumed to be the work of the loose animal but as with *Cat People* and *I Walked With a Zombie*, things are not quite what they seem. As things turn out, the killings of helpless young women are being perpetrated not by a wild beast but by a man "with a kink in his brain." Again, Tourneur turns out a suspenseful story punctuated by moody set pieces such as a little girl walking beneath a railroad trestle late at night and a young woman trapped within the walls of a cemetery on a second night. But despite those scenes and beautiful b/w cinematography by Robert De Grasse, the film is somewhat dull slowed down by extended sequences meant to fill out the personalities of the victims before they're killed. Nevertheless, a quiet, even thoughtful film, this is not your run of the mill horror movie…this is superior stuff!

Kiki Walker (Jean Brooks) adds something new to her nightclub act.

The first victim? So viewers were led to believe…

…but as the leopard's owner (Abner Biberman, right) tells Dennis O'Keefe, his trained pet wouldn't hurt a fly!

Curse of the Cat People (1944)

Sequel to 1942's *Cat People* is barely that with cat girl Simone Simon only appearing as a child's imaginary friend. Although Kent Smith and Jane Randolph return this time married with a small daughter, there's otherwise very little connection between this story of an introverted child with an active fantasy life and events in the first film. Instead, menace is presented in the form of a mother/daughter struggle which the little girl (Ann Carter) manages to reconcile by the end of the movie. Still, the indoor/outdoor sets are beautifully evocative on the order of those done for *I Walked With a Zombie* and quiet direction by Robert Wise (his first directorial effort aided by the cinematography of Val Lewton regular Nicholas Musuraca) moves the story along at a sedate pace. For completists only.

As dreamy as ever, Simone Simon (left) as the ghost of Irena from *Cat People* appears to Amy Reed (Ann Carter).

Cool scene emphasizing how Amy Reed's loneliness and inability to fit in isolates her both from the adult world and that of other children.

Creepy Elizabeth Russell as the disturbed and murderous Barbara Farren.

Robert Wise takes aim as first time director for *Curse of the Cat People*.

The Uninvited (1944)

Low key effort by director Lewis Allen and starring Ray Milland as Roderick Fitzgerald and Ruth Hussey as sister Pamela. The two siblings you see, fall in love with a big old house in England and, impressed by the unusually low price, decide to buy it. They soon discover the reason why it was so cheap: it's haunted! But don't start rolling your eyes. This film, at least was produced at a time before clichés about haunted house movies were very well established. In fact, this film was likely the first to take such a subject seriously as the siblings run into cold spots, hold seances, and have funny feelings about unseen presences. 1940s cinematography by Charles B. Lang is of the quality to be expected ie solid and Milland and Hussey are good in their rolls. But the overall pace is such that when the séance scene rolls around, modern audiences are likely to waver in their commitment to the film.

Alan Napier as Dr. Scott , Ray Milland, Gail Russel as Stella Meredith, and Ruth Hussey hold a séance in *The Uninvited*. **What's next? A Ouija board?**

You'd expect potential buyers to think twice about a house located this close to a cliff!

Frightened by the ghost, Gail Russell as Stella Meredith makes a suicidal dash to the cliff.

The Ghost and Mrs. Muir (1947)

Not exactly scary, this film comes more under the heading of fantasy than horror. Some humor peppers its otherwise serious story line about Gene Tierney as Lucy Muir, a widow who buys a remote seaside home that the local real estate agent finds difficult to sell. (And where have we heard *that* before?) But despite being told that it's haunted, Lucy decides to buy the house and moves in with young daughter Anna played by Natalie Wood. Soon, she encounters the former owner of the house, the ghost of a sea captain called Daniel Gregg (actually Rex Harrison). At first the demure widow and brash sea captain have a rough relationship but that soon settles down enough so that Lucy helps the Captain write and publish his autobiography. Along the way, Lucy is thwarted in love (she falls for a cad played by George Sanders, who else?) But her real love has always been the impossible one of the ghostly Captain. But the Captain has stopped haunting the house and as the years pass, Lucy grows older and finally convinces herself that the ghost was only a figment of her imagination. Until, one day, Anna returns with her fiancé and tells her mother about the imaginary friend she had when she was a little girl: the ghost of Captain Gregg. In a bittersweet ending, Lucy dies of old age and when she does, the Captain returns to take the hand of her spiritual self and lead her from the house and presumably into a happier afterlife. With incredible sets, gorgeous cinematography by Charles Lang, score by the great Bernard Herrmann, and direction by Joseph L. Mankiewicz how could a movie like this miss? Add romance and heartbreak and even a cosmic ending, and this one has it all!

Gene Tierney as Lucy Muir meets the ghost who haunts her new home.

The wooden marker pictured here was used to good effect in a montage indicating the passing of years during which Lucy becomes convinced she had only imagined knowing the ghost.

The ghost of Captain Gregg escorts Lucy's spirit from her lifeless body into eternity

Mighty Joe Young (1949)

Light-hearted, endearing fantasy of an oversized ape (billed in the credits as Mr. Joe Young!) and his pretty mistress, Jill Young played by Terry Moore. It seems that Jill has raised a gorilla from infancy to giant size (about 12 feet tall…not exactly King Kong dimensions, but scary enough when the beast gets loose in Hollywood of all places) and has caught the attention of nightclub owner Max O'Hara (played by Robert Armstrong reprising his role from *Kong* as an exploiter of giant apes). Seems Joe can help both Max and Jill by starring at the club and earning enough money to keep the former from going broke and the latter from losing her African ranch. But as to be expected, things go wrong and Joe escapes leaving destruction in his wake. But it was all unintended because Joe is really a kind hearted soul who ends up a hero when he rescues children from a burning orphanage. In addition to its status as a classic of the genre, *Mighty Joe Young* is also distinguished as the team up of stop motion master Willis O'Brien and protégé Ray Harryhausen. Unfortunately, O'Brien's career would dwindle after this film while that of Harryhausen would take off. As it is, this film is mostly a triumph for Harryhausen who did all the hands on work of animation while O'Brien concentrated mostly on the technical aspects of the film. Displaying a skill that would pave the way for his participation in later films, Harryhausen managed to infuse in a stop-motion puppet an amazing degree of personality that commands the viewer's sympathy.

Ray Harryhausen at work animating Joe for a scene in *Mighty Joe Young*.

Joe rescues a child from the burning orphanage.

Terry Moore when she starred in *Mighty Joe Young*.

Great composite shot by Harryhausen of Joe holding Jill (Terry Moore) over his head!

Destination Moon (1950)

Made in color, *Destination Moon* has the distinction of being the first attempt by Hollywood to produce a serious science fiction movie. And though the plot involving a space mission paid for and developed by private concerns does predict such companies as today's SpaceX, the story is marred by the presence of a crewmember included for what was considered "comic relief" but who simply keeps the film from being fully recommended. What it all adds up to is kinda dull despite being well served by excellent FX and the participation of SF writer Robert Heinlein. Produced by George Pal and directed by Irving Pichel, *Destination Moon* was intended as a realistic depiction of a trip to the moon, but events since have dated it badly. The speech upon landing however, does echo the words later uttered by Neal Armstrong claiming the moon in the name of all mankind "by the grace of God" and "the authority of the United States." The script, written among others by Heinlein (who also served as technical advisor and upon whose novel *Rocket Ship Galileo* the film was based), is well served with decent visuals such as the scenes of the rocket resting on the desert floor and paintings of the lunar surface by Chesley Bonestell. Interestingly, only a few years after this film was made, Heinlein made a second try at realism in space with a script for *Project Moonbase*. And although that film had considerably fewer resources money wise, it was the more entertaining film.

Very cool image of the rocket in *Destination Moon* coming in for a landing but it's design hardly predicted the look of the real world Lunar Landing Module that eventually made the trip to the Moon in 1969.

Science Fiction author Robert Heinlein and his wife on the set of *Destination Moon*.

NASA's Lunar Landing Module resting on the surface of the Moon.

The intrepid crew of *Destination Moon*. Unfortunately, there were no female members around to serve coffee. This was a realistic take on such a trip, remember?

Rocketship XM (1950)

Surprisingly good low budget entry intended at the time to beat more expensive *Destination Moon* into theaters. Irony is that despite lower cost, rushed production schedule, and questionable science, it's the superior film. The black and white photography is moody and effective giving the film a hard edged, realistic flavor especially in scenes aboard cramped quarters of the space ship and a shot of the crew as they make their way down a darkened corridor prior to blast off. Rocket ship sets are well done and special effects work within their limits. A night shot of the rocket sitting on its launch pad is good and matte shots on Mars very cool. Also cute is the red tint given the Martian settings. The Mars scenes are so effective in fact that it's a distinct let down when their spoiled by the needless appearance of a gang of primitive Martians. Warning to Earth about the perils of nuclear war is to be expected but not the unhappy ending where our hero Lloyd Bridges (as pilot Col. Floyd Graham) and attractive chemist Ossa Massen (as chemist Dr. Lisa Van Horn) are killed when the rocket runs out of fuel and crashes to Earth.

That's our crew for *Rocketship XM* including Ona Massen in the center and Lloyd Bridges second from right. Looking at the equipment they're sporting, including rifles and sidearms, it's anyone's guess what they were expecting to find on the Moon, their original destination!

The crew of *Rocketship XM* attend a press briefing prior to takeoff.

An off duty Dr. Lisa Van Horn (Osa Massen).

...and on the job as mission chemist!

The Day the Earth Stood Still (1951)

The Granddaddy of them all! This first of the post-World War II SF movies started the 50s off on a classy note and remains as one of the most loved, best remembered fantasy films of all time. Masterfully directed by Robert Wise with an atmospheric score by Bernard Hermann, the script is loosely based on a short story by Harry Bates ("Farewell to the Master") and follows the adventures of Klaatu (Michael Rennie), an alien sent to earth by the local galactic empire to warn humanity to change its violent ways or face "obliteration." Of course, the first thing that happens is that we shoot him! Later, Klaatu escapes from the hospital, befriends a young boy and his mother (Patricia Neal as Helen Benson) and, despite learning that the human race really isn't all that bad, still delivers his dire warning in the end. The robot that has accompanied him, you see, is a completely autonomous inter-galactic policeman who, acting as judge, jury, and executioner, rules the galaxy through terror! No matter how much Klaatu may sympathize with us, there's nothing he can do to alter the judgment of robots like Gort should they decide humanity is breaking galactic law. Despite all that however, Klaatu yet confirms his belief in a supreme being. When asked by Helen if Gort has the power over life and death, he assures her that "only the Almighty Spirit" has that power. A film that works on two levels, a warning against continued warfare in the atom age and a deeply human story as well, *Day the Earth Stood Still* continues to fascinate and enthrall by the wonder and terror of its ideas and what it has to say about being human: the good and the bad, the selflessness and the greed, the cynicism and the innocence. A gigantic, towering triumph in the cinema of the fantastic! PS Avoid the 2008 remake at all costs!

Klatuu, Barada, Nikto! Klatuu assures Helen that "only the Almighty Spirit" has the power over life and death.

Patricia Neal (Helen Benson) and Michael Rennie (Klatuu).

Billy Gray as Bobby Benson is a key element in helping Klatuu better understand the human condition.

Spectacular opening sequence of Klatuu's space ship coming in to land at a ball park on the Washington Mall! These scenes were crucial in establishing the believability and the almost documentary feel of *The Day the Earth Stood Still*.

The Thing (From Another World) (1951)

What a decade the 1950s was turning out to be! First, *Rocketship XM*, then *The Day the Earth Stood Still,* and now *The Thing!* Long suffering SF fans must have thought they were living right. And while the screenwriters for *Day the Earth Stood Still* did a decent job turning Harry Bates' original story into a film, every SF writer should have their work treated as well as *The Thing* treats John W. Campbell's short story "Who Goes There?" A seminal SF film that gets everything right, *The Thing* has it all: rapid-fire dialogue, fast moving direction (by Christian Nyby…or was it Howard Hawks?), good plot (based roughly on the first half of Campbell's classic tale), great cast (headed by one of our favorites, Kenneth Tobey!) and plenty of atmosphere (scientists and military men trapped in a few quonset huts at the top of the world during a snow storm with a blood-thirsty, shape-shifting alien running loose). Tobey as Capt. Patarick Hendry, takes over a North Pole research facility after a flying saucer ("We finally got one!") is found frozen in the ice. The military further clamps down when the body of the alien pilot is also discovered. Lead scientist Dr. Arthur Carrington (played by Robert Cornthwaite) protests but is outranked. Dialogue throughout is terse and realistic (funny too as when addressing relations between Hendry and girlfriend Nikki Nicholson played by Margaret Sheridan, on the scene as Carrington's secretary). Both this film and *Day the Earth Stood Still* established the military as trusted agents of authority in SF films for decades to come with stars like Kenneth Tobey and Craig Stevens lending it all an air of integrity. Iconic scene: where the men discover the flying saucer buried in the ice by moving out searching for its outline and ending up in the shape of a circle…all choreographed to the music of Dmitri Tiomkin! And remember: "Watch the Skies!" Avoid later remakes that miss the mark entirely.

Our man Kenneth Tobey whose handful of appearances in 50s SF movies was enough to cement his as the image of the indomitable spirit of the American cold warrior.

Margaret Sheridan: worthy of any red blooded American hero!

Iconic moment when the cast of *The Thing* realize what they've found frozen in the ice!

Climactic moment when James Arness (as the Thing) corners his human antagonists…or so he thinks! Moody cinematography by Russell Harlan.

When Worlds Collide (1951)

What?! Another top ranked SF film from 1951? It's true! While not quite reaching the quality of *Day the Earth Stood Still* or *The Thing*, *When Worlds Collide* has charms all its own including often spectacular FX, good story, and even metaphoric underpinnings. The film makes no attempt to disguise its source material (other than Philip Wylie's novel of the same name) when it opens and closes with quotes from the *Bible*. Essentially an update of the story of Noah's Ark, the film tells of the approach of a rogue star that threatens the destruction of the Earth. Scientists race against time and human frailty to build a rocket that will allow a select few to escape the Earth and start a new colony on a planet circling the approaching star! Sure it's hokum, but this George Pal production is laced with fine FX including the flooding of New York City. However, the rocket is the real star of the show and shots of it while under construction are particularly nice. The movie is also helped along by a pleasant cast including the lovely Barbara Rush (as Joyce Hendron, whose father heads up the escape project), Richard Derr (as David Randall, the lucky gopher who manages to attach himself to the escape project, get a place on the rocket, and win the girl), and Larry Keating (as Dr. Cole Hendron, the unlucky guy who loses Joyce to Larry). Scenes depicting the desperate race against time to complete the rocket and escape the endangered Earth are still compelling. Fun!

Great shot of the rocket while under construction. Matting in of live action and model work is flawless throughout these scenes from *When Worlds Collide*.

Barbara Rush: who wouldn't want to be marooned on a deserted planet with her?

Lucky Richard Derr!

FX personnel work on the rocket set for *When Worlds Collide*.

War of the Worlds (1953)

Now we're getting to the heart of the order! A near perfect SF film. And why not? It's cribbed from H. G. Wells' literary masterpiece of the same name! Moving from the local to the global, the plot develops quickly as our stoic scientist hero played by Gene Barry (as Dr. Clayton Forrester) makes his way through inter-planetary battle scenes, municipal carnage, and the hazards of romance (with Ann Robinson as Sylvia van Buren) to finally see the Martian villains succumb to Earth's nasty bacteria! Produced by George Pal and directed by Byron Haskin, the movie is nearly all filmed on soundstages and backlots with traditional FX that unfortunately reveal themselves in the wiring needed to support the heavy Martian fighters. All that and the film even manages a religious sub-text and a great pre credit intro narrated by Cedric Hardwick! And who can forget such scenes as the Martian ships emerging from an atomic blast protected by their transparent blisters of solidified force, or Los Angeles reduced to smoking rubble, or heroine Anne Robinson's reaching the breaking point when it's discovered that even the Martian machines (gulp) bleed? We can't! But beware the 2005 remake. Why bother with junk made just yesterday when you have the original to drool over?

Cool shot of Martian fighters emerging from the canister that rocketed them to Earth. *War of the Worlds* was shot in color as most A list studio genre films were during the 1950s making for far more stunning visuals than presented here in b/w.

Our hero and heroine: Gene Barry and Anne Robinson as Dr. Clayton Forrester and Sylvia van Buren respectively.

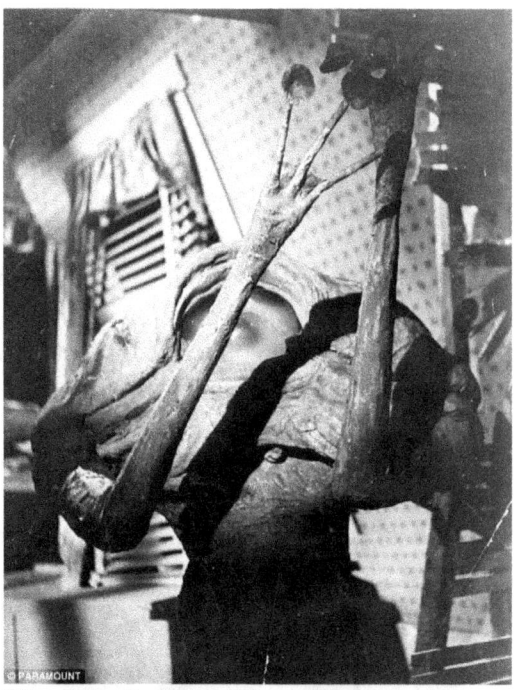

The Martians in *War of the Worlds* are only shown briefly but here's a still that you can study at leisure!

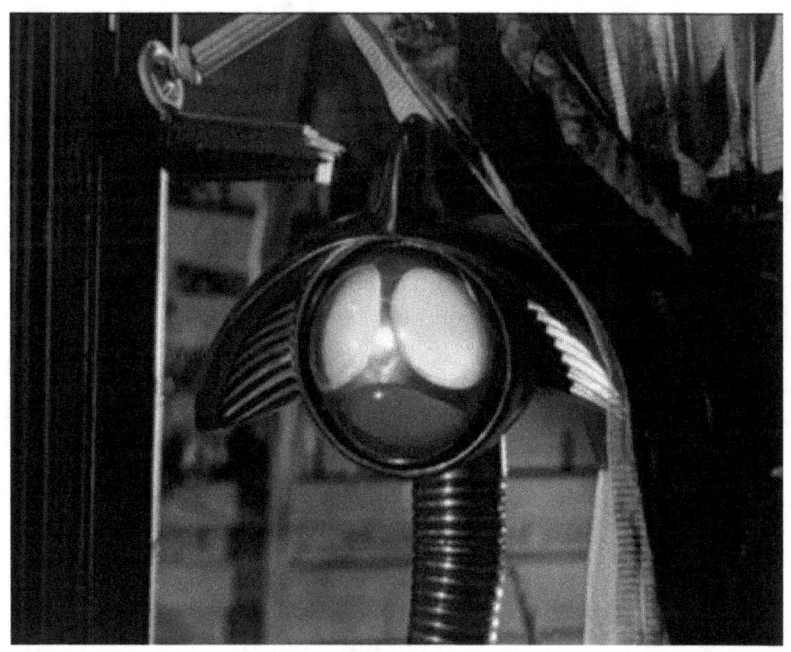

What Sylvia van Buren saw: a Martian periscope type device…that bleeds!

The Beast From 20,000 Fathoms (1953)

One of the crown jewels of 50s SF; a literate, fast moving script by Fred Freiberger and Louis Morheim does a good job expanding upon Ray Bradbury's short story "The Foghorn" that the movie is based on. Directed by Eugene Lourie (who had the good wisdom not to interfere with FX wizard Ray Harryhausen), the film includes a terrific opening at the North Pole and mounting suspense punctuated by the celebrated attack by the Beast on a lonely lighthouse before the action climaxes in New York City. There, the US Army moves in eventually corralling the creature within the Coney Island roller coaster for a fiery finish. Harryhausen's first solo feature as FX creator is also possibly his best with combined stop motion miniature, rear screen, and matte shots making for amazing and seamless scenes of destruction by an aroused prehistoric Beast. Only question mark is casting of Paul Christian (nee Paul Hubschmid) in the lead. His obvious accent begs the question: was he supposed to be one of those German scientists recruited by the US after World War II? Regardless, the film also features the great Kenneth Tobey, king of 50s SF cinema!

In a by now familiar scene to fantasy fans, the Beast rampages through the streets of New York.

The money shot: the Beast about to lay waste the lighthouse!

The scene that disturbed the bejeezus out this viewer when he first saw it! The Beast swallows a hapless police officer!

Not your average SF movie stars: Paula Raymond as Lee Hunter and Paul Christian as Prof. Tom Nesbitt.

It Came From Outer Space (1953)

1953 was turning out to be another banner year for SF fans! First, *War of the Worlds*, then *Beast From 20,000 Fathoms*, and now another classic to be: *It Came From Outer Space*! A fun story by science fiction great Ray Bradbury, some of whose original script actually survives in a final version written by Harry Essex. The idea of aliens taking over human beings in a small desert town might sound familiar, but hold the phone! They're not here to take over the world, but just to repair their damaged space craft. Moody direction by monster movie master Jack Arnold turns this one into gold. Check out his deft touch in the scene in the desert where the telephone lineman tells how sometimes he hears strange things out there all by himself followed by weird sounds and a shot of the telephone wires as they run to the horizon: was it just the wind or what? The scene is accompanied by dialogue that must have survived from Bradbury's original script as telephone lineman Joe Sawyer speaks them in a natural yet evocative delivery sure to send chills down your spine! Other such snatches of dialogue are sprinkled throughout the film adding just the right touch of…dare I say it? mysticism to the goings on. Starring genre regulars Richard Carlson (as John Putnam, the writer that no one believes saw a spacecraft at the bottom of a newly formed meteorite crater) and Russell Johnson (as George, a telephone lineman taken over by aliens with a penchant for staring into the sun), accompanied by lovely Barbara Rush (as Putnam's fiancé, Ellen Fields, fresh off of *When Worlds Collide*). A must see!

Classic FX shot of half buried alien craft from *It Came From Outer Space*.

Barbara Rush doesn't look too interested here, but this shot was filmed to take advantage of the film's 3D production values.

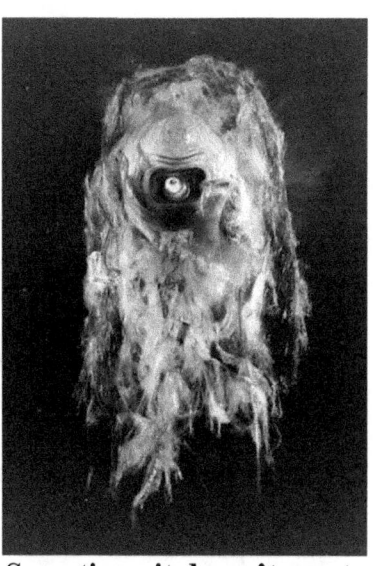

Sometimes it doesn't pay to get too good a look at the monster...

Shot from eerie scene when Richard Carlson learns a lesson from Frank Daylon (Joe Sawyer) about the isolated life of telephone linemen working in the desert. In a number of his 50s SF movies, director Jack Arnold used desert locations to establish mood and atmosphere, isolating his characters in a landscape that seemed every bit as strange and foreign as any alien planet.

Joe Sawyer as lineman Frank Daylon, listens as the wires "sing and hum and whisper"

The Magnetic Monster (1953)

Most Sf fans likely missed this "scientific procedural" that often felt more like a government educational film of the 50s than a regular movie. Directed by Curt Siodmak, it starred Richard Carlson as Dr. Jeffrey Stewart who, together with partner Dr. Dan Forbes (King Donovan. Gotta love that name!) who become science detectives as they track down the source of a new radioactive isotope that has displayed some disturbing properties including uncontrolled growth and the release of magnetic energy. The ultimate danger is that the new isotope will absorb enough energy to alter the Earth's rotation and even throw it from orbit. What to do? The movie is distinguished by the use of actual locations and authentic looking lab equipment including a computer called MANIAC! In fact, no one watching this absorbing little film could tell that it was shot in a mere 11 days. Whatever other attention it needed was presumably taken up in post production when the rather limited but well done FX were put in (shots of the radioactive isotope under microscopes were particularly effective). The film is also unique among most SF movies in that the "monster" of the title is never seen (except under the aforementioned microscope). Not so Jean Byron as Connie Stewart, Jeffrey's wife who adds some needed humanity to the dire goings on. Although the integration is pretty flawless, one drawback of the film is its extensive use of stock material in its final scenes from an old German silent called *Gold*. Luckily for genre fans though, this film was likely a lot more interesting than that earlier epic!

Ivan Tors, who produced *Magnetic Monster*, went on to develop the more well known *Flipper* TV series!

Pretty Jean Byron gave *Magnetic Monster* a human dimension and Richard Carlson a good reason to hurry up and get back home!

Not exactly an action shot, but this capture of Richard Carlson as Dr. Jeffrey Stewart heading to his lab illustrates what location shooting can do for a low budget film. In *Magnetic Monster* in particular, they not only saved money, they contributed to the film's sense of *verite*

King Donovan and Richard Carlson don the hazmat suits to track down the "magnetic monster."

The Twonky (1953)

Included here because you can never go wrong when you adapt a classic SF story…well, almost never! Loose and whimsical adaptation of the story by Henry Kuttner and wife C.L. Moore (writing together under the pseudonym of Lewis Padgett), produced independently and directed by Arch Oboler. Extremely low budget and not very well acted, the film updates the story's radio/twonky to a television set. Worth of your time only if you're a die hard fan of the original short story.

One of the low budget FX shots as the "Twonky" helps light Hans Conried's cigarettes.

Before he turned to movies, Arch Oboler directed episodes of the radio show *Lights Out*.

Henry Kuttner and wife C.L. Moore were both giants in the golden age of magazine science fiction before they married and became Lewis Padgett

Connie Marshall, who played football team cheerleader Susie, had a long career in film and TV before and after *The Twonky*.

Hans Conried, as hapless suburbanite Kerry West, loses it. *The Twonky* of the title is a device from another dimension that only looks like a TV set accidently delivered to West. From there, its programming takes over as it tries to control West's life and have it conform to the authoritarian world from which it originates.

Project Moonbase (1953)

At first glance, viewers might be justified in dismissing this low low budget entry by director Richard Talmadge as Buck Rogers type hokum (secret plots by unnamed enemy powers, hot pants sporting astronettes, etc) but on closer inspection they'd find something a little more intriguing. That's because the script was written by science fiction writer Robert A. Heinlein who, within the film's restrictive budget, attempts to depict what life in space and a trip to the Moon might really be like. Heinlein's idiosyncrasies can be spotted in a number of places including the film's noble attempt to overcome bare bones special effects and depict the realities of space. It's depiction of the NASA-like delivery of a lunar landing module to the surface of the Moon and how it would communicate with the Earth while stranded on the dark side is noteworthy. Other details include the wonders of weightlessness as characters walk and sit on ceilings and walls in an orbiting space station (complete with signs with writing both upside down and rightside up!) and don comfortable dress for shipboard life including shorts, T-shirts, and even skullcaps designed to keep hair in place in a zero g environment (the hot pants style shorts are especially appealing on cute Donna Martell!). With all that, it's ironic that even though many of the film's scientific aspects have not proven completely accurate, its underlying social context has become increasingly familiar with the rise of political correctness. For instance, Heinlein's proto-feminism depicted for the year 1970 (!) includes a female president and a woman being the first American in orbit (albeit due to her weight rather than her gender…later, the female president insists that Martell's Col. Breiteis [pronounced "bright-eyes"] also pilot the first mission to the Moon). Traditional American values however, are upheld when Breiteis and her male co-pilot Maj. Bill Moore (played by the wooden Ross Ford), finding themselves stranded on the Moon for weeks, are compelled to wed by Earth authorities! As fun as it is, *Project Moonbase* is still a third tier film but gets an A for effort and the number of SF concepts crammed into its brief 63 minute running time.

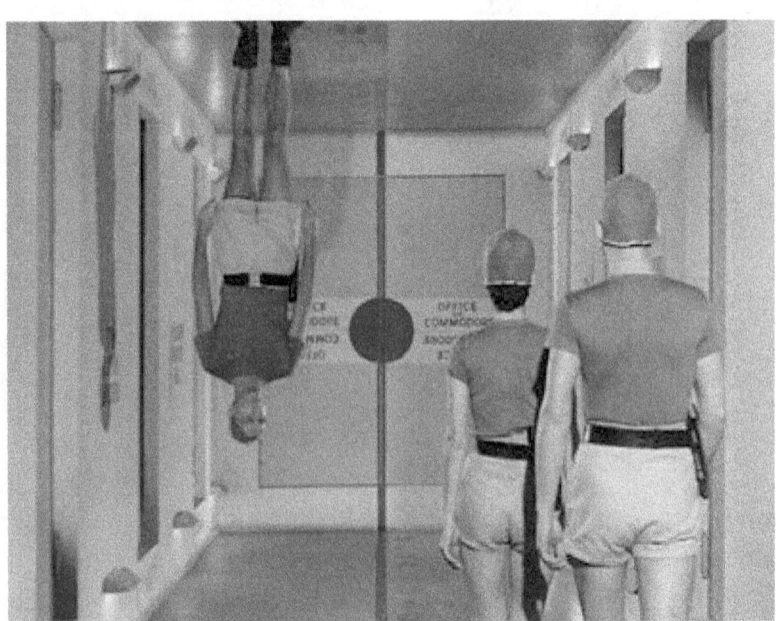

Life aboard a space station in *Project Moonbase*!

Before *Star Wars*, female leads in SF movies were required to be eye catching as well as brainy and Donna Martell (Col. Breiteis) sure fit the bill!

Science fiction writer Robert A. Heinlein.

Nice miniature work and use of rear screen projection here.

Invaders From Mars (1953)

Minimalist sets, psychological color tones, and expressionistic direction by William Cameron Menzies ought to add up to the mother of all childhood nightmares but falls short. A circular plot and scenes with soldiers chasing Martians through an endless series of tunnels, vitiates the film's initial impact. But still, there's lots of fun along the way!

Viewers knew something was not quite right with *Invaders From Mars* after this loopy scene in which Jimmy Hunt (as young David MacLean) and Arthur Franz (as Dr. Stuart Kelston) matter of factly discuss how the aliens likely came from Mars!

Lovely Helena Carter played child psychologist Dr. Patricia Blake in *Invaders From Mars*.

Helen Carter is prepared for a lobotomy by the Martians!

Jimmy Hunt (as David MacLean) shows the troops how to use a Martian disintegrator. That's Morris Ankrum, a 50s SF film standby, as the general in charge right behind Hunt.

Set designer William Cameron Menzies maximizes a lean budget by minimizing sets and using them to reflect characters' anxieties. Here, a long, forced perspective hallway seems to reflect young David MacLean's growing isolation from a distrustful adult world.

Them! (1954)

The first and best of the giant bug movies is also extremely well done! Who can forget that first, chilling glimpse of the giant ant hill in the middle of the desert, swathed in wind driven sand? Or the perilous descent into the ant hill with gas masks, flashlights, machine guns, and flame throwers? Or what about the scores of jeeps thundering through the Los Angeles sewer system looking for the giant ant colony? Or the chill we all felt that first time we heard the strange ant call whistling on the desert wind outside the wrecked general store (with shadows wheeling crazily from a swinging lamp)? Answer: nobody! Those scenes will be forever implanted in our brains thanks to George Worthing Yates who came up with the story and Ted Sherdeman who scripted it. Direction by Gordon Douglas is flawless. Almost convincing ant FX is lent believability by a fine cast led by James Whitmore, James Arness, and Edmund Gwenn each determined to take it all seriously. Joan Weldon, first of a line of realistic lady scientists, is a genuine feminist icon. Add it all up and it spells classic!

The extended sequence of James Whitmore, James Arness, and Joan Weldon making their way through mist laden tunnels inside the ant hill to the egg chamber is one of the most unforgettable in SF cinema history!

James Arness as FBI agent Robert Graham, Joan Weldon as entomologist Pat Medford, James Whitmore as police Sgt. Ben Peterson, and Edmund Gwenn as Dr. Harold Medford. Casting for *Them* was crucial if the producers were to convince audiences of the reality of giant ants and this lineup delivered!

The army moves out! Shots with scores of jeeps driving through the L.A. sewer system looking for giant ants was another memorable sequence in *Them*. Scenes involving the military coming to the rescue became routine in SF films of the 50s.

This Island Earth (1954)

SF tale with interesting hook: aliens looking for qualified Earth scientists send them a test in the form of having to build an all purpose communication device called an "interociter!" If the scientist manages to get it built and contacts the aliens, he's qualified for abduction! Directed by Jack Arnold from a tale by sci fi writer Raymond Jones, the story tells of aliens from the planet Metaluna who need help from Earth scientists to devise a defense against enemies trying to destroy their home world. An ambitious film that brings together a range of SF concepts including mutants, space travel, interstellar war, and tractor beams all presented in colors that jump off the screen. Opening scenes perfectly capture the can do spirit of the 1950s with scientist Rex Reason as comfortable in the cockpit of a jet as he is in the lab. When challenged by the alien leader about the place of Terrans in the scheme of the universe, Reason unerringly declares that "Our true size is the size of our God!" Nice FX sometimes show their age, but with a stellar cast headed by Reason (Dr. Cal Meachum) and sci fi veterans Jeff Morrow (as Metalunan point man Exeter), Russell Johnson (as Steve Carlson), and space vixen and Howard Hughes gal pal Faith Domergue (as Ruth Adams) on hand, it hardly matters!

The money shot: The alien ship bearing Cal Meachum and Ruth Adams prepares to leave war ravaged Metaluna! Look closely and you can spot the figures of Cal and Ruth walking seamlessly through a combination matte shot and live action.

Rex Reason as Dr. Cal Meachum was a new kind of cinema scientist, not mad, but heroic, encompassing all of the virtues of 1950s manliness: smart, with a military background, and God fearing. Here, he briefs reporters on his latest research while suiting up to fly a fighter jet to his lab!

Glamorous Faith Domergue made her mark in a number of genre films. Besides *This Island Earth*, she also starred in *It Came From Beneath the Sea* and *Cult of the Cobra*. Here, she looks as if she's ready for her next SF assignment!

FX personnel work on the Metalunan planetscape for *This Island Earth*.

Creature from the Black Lagoon (1954)

Director Jack Arnold strikes again with a vehicle that keeps your interest from the moment that webbed hand is found sticking out of the side of a rock formation to the final scene where we see the Gill Man's batraic form slowly sink into the murky waters of the lagoon. In fact, there are so many cool things about this trend setting monster/SF film that it's hard to know where to start listing them! There's the infamous three chord monster theme by Joseph Gershenson (ta da daaaa!), the opening narration quoting from Genesis (ending with those creepy webbed footprints emerging from the sea), crystal clear underwater photography by James C. Havens and Scotty Welbourne, first rate creature effects, and of course, the choreographed swimming scene with Julia Adams is justifiably famous (even when one considers its dubious Freudian connotations!) Like *It Came From Outer Space, Creature* also features a lean script complete with sequences of moody monologues by the hero evoking the strangeness of the environment depicted in the film and the universe in general, an Arnold trademark. Finally, it features a stellar cast, each of whom would become increasingly familiar in the fantastic films of the 50s: Richard Carlson in the lead (as Dr. David Reed), Richard Denning (Dr. Mark Williams) as the rich financier of the expedition and rival for the affections of Carlson's main squeeze, the radiant Kay Lawrence (Julia Adams, unforgettable in a pair of white short shorts!) In fact, everything in this classic B picture shouts that it should rank as nothing short of an A!

Is it Freudian or isn't it? You be the judge as the Creature mirrors Kay's strokes while she takes a swim in the Black Lagoon. Lucky for viewers, she wasn't worried about piranhas or alligators!

Yummy Julie Adams in the iconic white swimsuit. At this point, the threatening Creature is only incidental!

A good cast makes for a great movie: Whit Bissell as Dr. Ewin Thompson, Julie Adams as Kay Lawrence, Richard Denning as Dr. Mark Williams, and Richard Carlson as Dr. David Reed. All would become familiar faces in 50s SF cinema.

Target Earth (1954)

An interesting premise involving army of Venusian robots attacking an unnamed American city falls short due to budget constraints. Genre regular Richard Denning as Frank Brooks, heads a small cast of characters left behind after the city has been evacuated who are forced to hole up in an abandoned hotel as death dealing robots roam the streets. A film whose grasp well exceeded its reach nevertheless does a decent job with limited resources by concentrating on interpersonal relationships rather than FX. When one of the robots finally appears it's all too obvious why it was kept under wraps so long: a good shove is all it would take to knock it over! The film does have an interesting opening as heroine Kathleen Crowley, as Nora King, wakes from a failed suicide attempt to find herself alone in the city. The film was adapted from the novelette by SF writer Paul W. Fairman and is surprisingly faithful. For fanatics only!

One of the invading Venusian robots finally makes its appearance in *Target Earth*.

Kathleen Crowley and Richard Denning share a quiet moment in *Target Earth*. Wisely, characterization was emphasized over FX, just as it was in the novelette.

Virtually the entire cast of *Target Earth*: Kathleen Crowley, Richard Denning, Richard Reeves as Jim Wilson, and Virginia Adams as Vicki Harris.

Kathleen Crowley as Nora King runs through the streets of a deserted Los Angeles after waking up from an attempted suicide.

Cult of the Cobra (1955)

With genre faves Marshall Thompson and Faith Domergue, how can you go wrong? Answer: you can't! Not even with this slight but fun horror yarn about a female were-cobra being sicced on a group of hapless (not to mention culturally insensitive) American soldiers after they crash a snake worship ceremony in a nameless Asiatic country. Loaded with future TV stars such as Richard Long and Edward Platt. Low budgeter filmed mostly on sets and back lot, nevertheless manages to snag some atmosphere with nice b/w cinematography. Most effective in scenes with future *Fugitive* David Janssen as owner of a local bowling alley!

Cultural sensitivity was unknown in the 1950s when Marshall Thompson (shown here as Tom Markel) and his buddies break up a local religious ceremony (so what if they worship a snake god?) and incur *The Curse of the Cobra*!

Worshipper mimics the moves of a snake during cult ceremony attended by Marshall Thompson and his buddies.

Because you can never get enough of Faith Domergue: the MO of her character as the were-cobra was to seduce and then kill the men who violated the temple of the snake worshippers. They never had a chance!

Faith Domergue as Lisa Moya eyes her next victim...

Tarantula (1955)

Another offering from the hand of director Jack Arnold who again takes us into the desert where the action begins with people falling victim to a mysterious disease that really, has little to do with the main plot. John Agar stars as country doctor Matt Hastings when a tarantula filled with a test serum escapes from an isolated lab run by Prof. Gerald Deemer played by Leo G. Carroll. As the film progresses, so does the spider, growing quickly into a hairy behemoth. Along the way, it kills cattle, ranchers, and hobos in that order building suspense until the final, thrilling climax when the Air Force comes to the rescue! Again composer Joseph Gershenson helps with the mood while Agar evokes the desert's mystery with a little speech to science student Mara Corda (as lab assistant Stephanie Clayton). Although special effects of the tarantula are by way of filming a real spider and enlarging rather than stop motion, skillful compositioning with miniatures and mattes is the best ever for this kind of work. Most of the FX shots are amazingly flawless making for a fun movie with a couple genuine moments of creepiness.

Mara Corday sans lab coat: not your average lab assistant!

Integration of enlarged images of a tarantula with live location shots were the most flawless of their kind and went a long way to enable a suspension of belief in *Tarantula*

John Agar examines Leo G. Carroll's unusual medical condition (to say the least) as Mara Corday looks on.

It Came From Beneath the Sea (1955)

Stunning Ray Harryhausen FX, sultry Faith Domergue and best of all, Kenneth Tobey: what else could any 50s b-movie lover want? How about the perfect giant monster script involving an overgrown octopus terrorizing San Francisco? Or fast moving, suspenseful plot? Or mostly on location shooting giving everything a realistic, documentary feel? Truly deserving to be counted among the small circle of 50s classics!

Incredible Ray Harryhausen stop motion effects hardly hints at the fact that *It Came From Beneath the Sea* was his first full length solo feature. Fun fact: because of the low budget, there wasn't enough money for Harryhausen to articulate eight arms that a normal octopus has so producers had to get by with only six. Can you notice any difference?

Another shot of Harryhausen's octopus as it reaches across an empty beach

Sweet! Two of our fave 50s genre performers together in the same movie! Kenneth Tobey's Commander Pete Mathews puts the moves on Faith Domergue's Prof. Leslie Joyce.

It Came From Beneath the Sea took location shooting to new heights with some action taking place on a genuine submarine. Here's Kenneth Tobey on the bridge as Commander Pete Mathews

Revenge of the Creature (1955)

Cute Lori Nelson fills in very nicely for Julie Adams in *Revenge of the Creature*.

A strong followup to the original *Creature From the Black Lagoon* with Jack Arnold back in the director's chair. Good cast headed by John Agar on the reverse slope of his career and Lori Nelson filling in the white bathing suit quite nicely in place of Julia Adams! Freudian elements of the first film are treated somewhat heavy handedly this time around with repeat of famous swim scene between Gill Man and Nelson. Underwater photography is once again the FX highlight with musical director Joseph Gershenson again lending his three note monster theme to the mix. No new ground is explored but the movie is still entertaining with interesting set where Gill Man is held captive in a Florida aquarium.

John Agar trips the light fantastic with Lori Nelson just before she's nabbed by the Creature!

Love at first sight. The Gillman sets eyes on Helen Dobson *en dishabille* played by Lori Nelson. Can you blame him?

Sexual frustration?
Stock shot of the Gillman going into action as he escapes from the aquarium.

The Atomic Man (1955)

Director Ken Hughes takes his time telling this story about a man found floating in the harbor with a bullet in his back. Oh, and the body is also glowing! Turns out that the man is not dead but when he recovers, is unintelligible to everyone when he tries to speak. Reporter Mike Delaney (played by Gene Nelson) suspects a story and begins to investigate joined eventually by long suffering girlfriend Jill Rabowski (played by genre regular Faith Domergue). Why Nelson's character would rather be chasing a story than Domergue's Rabowski is anyone's guess but pursue the story he does until finally figuring out that the man in the hospital is somehow living seven and half seconds in the future and that everything he's been saying has been impossible to understand because he's answering questions before they've been put to him! Cool sci-fi concept was brainchild of author Charles Eric Maine who wrote the script for *Timeslip*, as *Atomic Man* was originally titled in the United Kingdom where it was shot. The novel from which the script was adapted was called *The Isotope Man*…confused yet? Aside from the idea of a man living a few seconds ahead in time, the movie is light on science fiction but makes up for it by claiming the distinction of being the first if not the only film noir SF movie ever made. For completists or Faith Domergue watchers only.

A sleuthing we will go. Faith Domergue as Jill Rabowski takes a snap as reporter/boyfriend Mike Delaney, played by Gene Nelson, looks on.

The action intensifies in *The Atomic Man* as hoods lean on an uncooperative scientist.

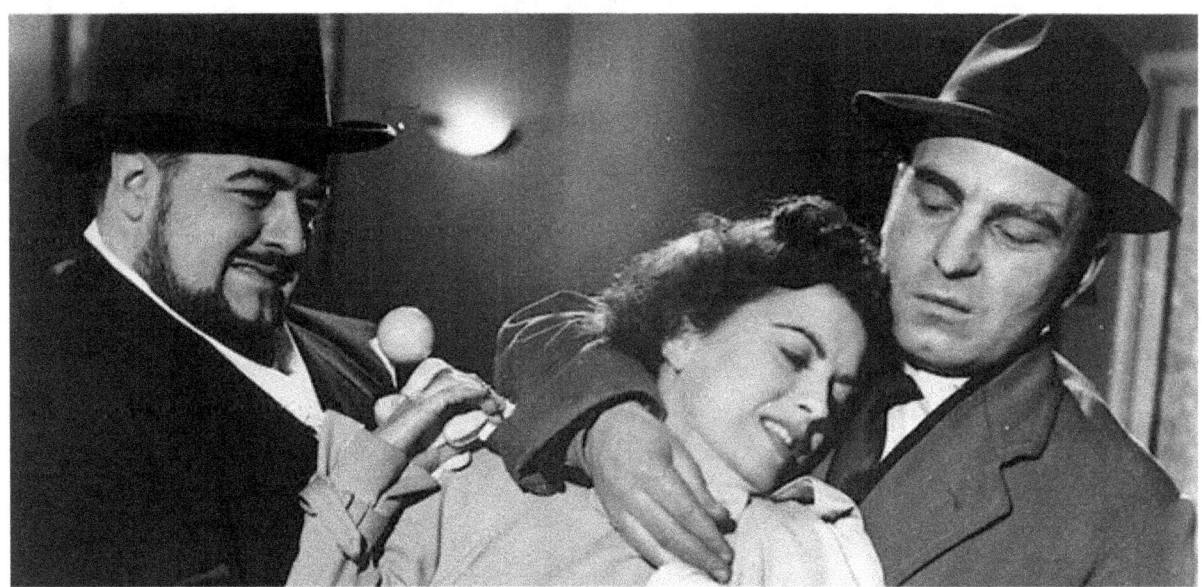

Faith Domergue as Jill Rabowski gets manhandled as she and Gene Nelson get too close to the truth.

Conquest of Space (1955)

The exception that proves the rule. A major pre *Star Wars* era SF film that falls flat. Despite overall impressive special effects, the story is humdrum punctuated with tedious instances of what is supposed to be humor. A bold attempt by producer George Pal and director Byron Haskin to imagine what an actual trip to Mars might look like (based on a book by Chesley Bonestell and Willy Ley), whatever post-war optimism the film derives from exploring the high frontier is mitigated by an inexplicable anti-religious streak unusual for movies of the era. More interesting for fans of the genre is the presence in the cast of three future stars of long running television series: Eric Fleming of *Rawhide*, William Hopper of *Perry Mason*, and Ross Martin of the *Wild Wild West*!

The crew gathers at the space station prior to their mission into deep space. Notice their meal in pill form. The film at least attempted a realistic depiction of what life in space would be like.

The crew takes their first close up look at the surface of Mars.

Often cool FX highlight *Conquest of Space* which are much more impressive in color.

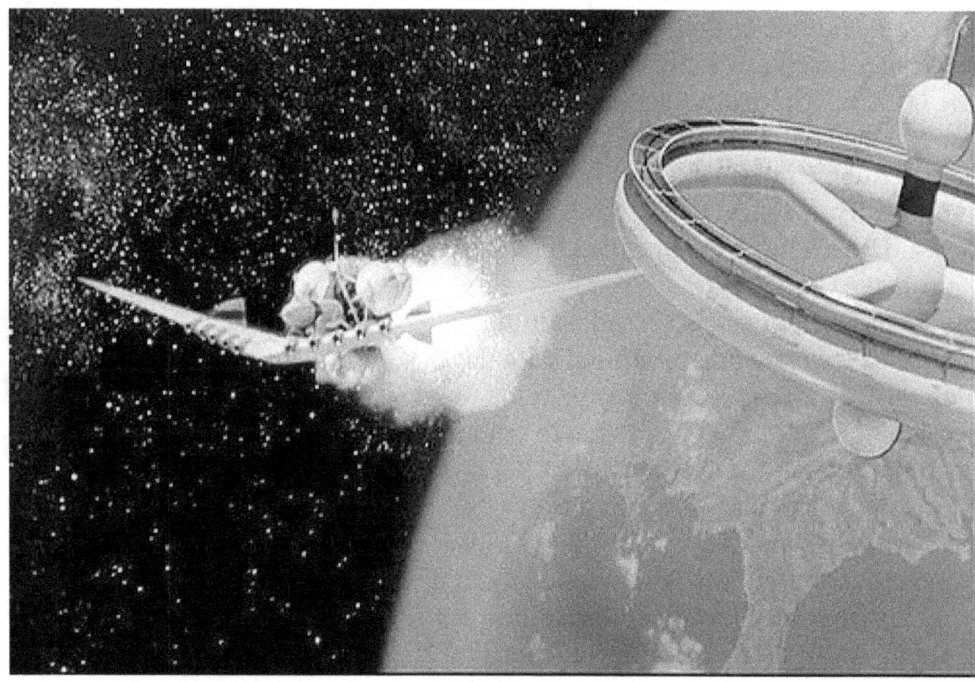

The *Conquest of Space* has begun! Another spectacular FX shot that is much more impressive in the technicolor the film was shot in.

Forbidden Planet (1956)

What can be said about the best science fiction film ever made but Wow! Okay, that's not enough to recommend it, but what about that plot: Shakespeare's *The Tempest* overlaid with intergalactic space patrols, vanished alien races, alien technologies on a grand scale, genetic engineering, Freudian psychology, and the lesson that no matter how far he may go, or how advanced technologically he may become, if man is unable to conquer his inner demons, it will all be for nothing. "We are, after all, not God," as commander John. J. Adams (played by Leslie Nielsen) sums it up for Altaira Morbius (played by the radiantly youthful Anne Francis) in the final line of perhaps the perfect science fiction film. And as if all that wasn't enough, there's also those great special effects, a good script and direction, and fine casting. Walter Pidgeon as Dr. Walter Morbius, Walter Stevens as Lt. Doc Ostrow, Richard Anderson as Chief Quinn, Earl Holliman, as the cook, and of course, Robbie the Robot. The first SF movie where really, no expense was spared and it shows! Especially in the breathtaking opening shots as the C-57D Earth cruiser makes its initial approach to Altair IV and later, the interior of the planet that's stuffed with the unearthly technology of the alien Krell. Everything was created from scratch with no location shooting…even the music, "electronic tonalities," was composed specifically for the film by Bebe and Louis Baron. Disney was brought in especially to do the animation work for the invisible monster of the Id. Talk about your icing on the cake! If you see only one sci fi movie in your life, this is the one!

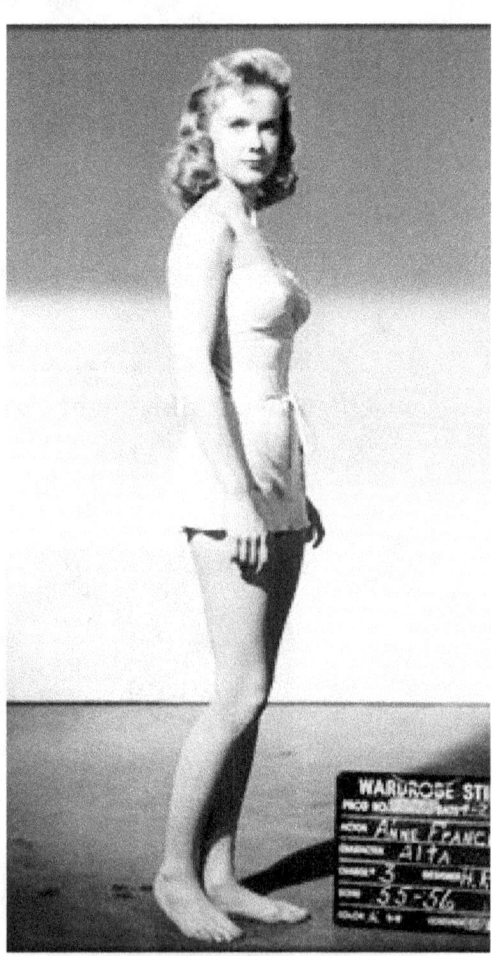

Yes, Anne Francis will do!

The invisible creature of the Id becomes visible in this screen capture animated by Disney FX artists with ray blasts outlining its energy form!

The wonders of the Krell. Morbius gives Commander Adams the grand tour of the subterranean Krell Id machine.

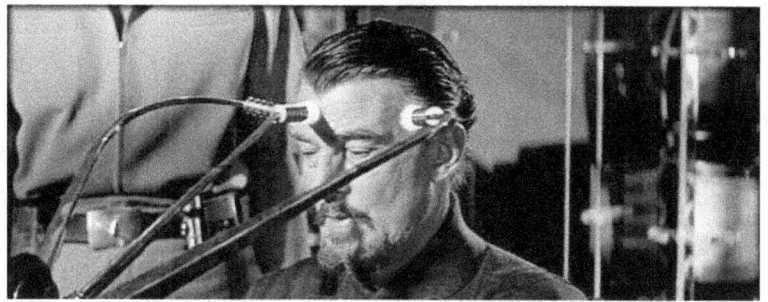

Morbius shows how the Id machine works

Invasion of the Body Snatchers (1956)

Although frequently claimed as being a cold war fable filled to the brim with our parents' supposed paranoias regarding the communist threat and the A-bomb, *Invasion of the Body Snatchers* is nothing of the kind. Granted, it has an underlying theme of the value of human emotions (when hero Kevin McCarthy is informed by the aliens that once replaced, he would feel no love, no desire, no faith, he replies "I'll have no part of it!"), but mostly this film is a solid adaptation of the novel by Jack Finney which, sub-text aside, is a rollicking good SF thriller of mounting suspense! Shot in crisp black and white, Don Siegel's direction transforms the sleepy town of Santa Mira into a beachhead for an alien invasion from space. Strangely, however, as the years move on and the increasingly intolerant culture of political correctness manifests itself, the values of the pod people become more and more relevant.

The last human beings left in Santa Mira, Kevin McCarthy as Dr. Miles Bennell and Dana Wynter as Becky Driscoll keep one step ahead of alien body doubles as they try to escape town to warn the world of the invasion. The scenes leading up to this point, from the seemingly inconsequential to outright ominous makes *Invasion of the Body Snatchers* a masterpiece of mounting suspense.

King Donovan! Here he is in left foreground, playing Bennell's friend Jack Belicec, the first to find a human replica growing on his pool table of all place. That's Carolyn Jones as Theodora Belicec biting her knuckles behind Kevin McCarthy, and Dana Wynter behind King Donovan

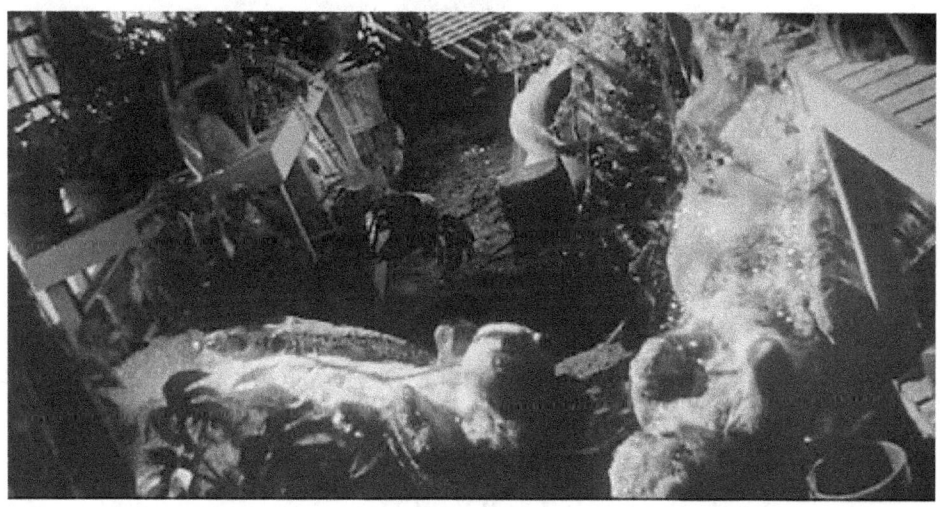

There is nothing to fear...pods bursting open with half formed replicas of Bennell, Driscoll, and the Belicecs spilling out.

Earth vs the Flying Saucers (1956)

Okay, so it's more or less a remake of *War of the Worlds* (it even features the same shot of the Los Angeles City Hall being blown up!), but with eye popping FX by Ray Harryhausen, who outdoes himself with inanimate objects this time out instead of dinosaurs, more than make up for it! In particular, matte shots of the saucers flying over ruined airbases, burning forests, and capital cities of the world are more than just impressive. Plus, latest releases of this film and other Harryhausen movies include colorized versions that look exactly as if they were shot that way, enhance the viewing experience. Add to that domestic scenes between stars Hugh Marlowe as Dr. Russell Marven and Joan Taylor as Carol Marvin, ancient aliens encased in exo-armor, and electric force fields, and you've got the makings of a classic SF film that's loads of fun!

A saucer crashes in the Capitol building! Harryhausen outdid himself for *Earth vs the Flying Saucers*, not only animating the saucers but every little chunk of masonry that crumbles from smashed monuments. Just amazing to contemplate when watching the movie!

Joan Taylor was the latest in a long line of attractive girlfriends, wives, or yes, even scientists that made classic SF cinema worth watching.

Hugh Marlowe was also a familiar face in SF cinema. Handsome and intense, he could be equally versatile as a hero or a heavy.

Ray Harryhausen in his studio working on a scene from *Earth Vs the Flying Saucers*. In many ways, animating inanimate objects such as the saucers and exploding buildings was one of Harryhausen's toughest assignments.

The Creature Walks Among Us (1956)

Jack Arnold was missing from the credits for this third sequel to the successful Gill Man series but director John Sherwood does a good job in maintaining the overall quality of the Creature films. Again, solid underwater photography bolsters the otherwise humdrum plot that involves using the Gill Man in experiments to create a hybrid form of humanity capable of withstanding the rigors of outer space. Interestingly, the figures of Jeff Morrow as a pre-war era mad scientist and Rex Reason as the more heroic post-war researcher set up a nice contrast between opposing definitions of the scientist that became the norm for SF films of the 50s and 60s. The evil, ethically challenged scientist would make a return only in the post-Watergate era when the public's suspicion of the government began to run high. In the meantime, though, Sherwood presents viewers with all the familiar tropes of the Creature films: penetration of the Amazonian swamps, pursuit of the Gill Man underwater, the white bathing suited form of the female lead (Leigh Snowdon is appealing but not in league with her predecessors Julia Adams or Lori Nelson!), and the Gill Man going wild as he escapes from his captors. An overlay of soap opera among the lead characters adds some depth to the story but fails to add excitement to the last third of the film. Fun Fact: This wasn't the first time Morrow and Reason, both vets of 50s SF movies, teamed up! They first appeared together in *This Island Earth*!

Leigh Snowdon as Marcia Barton does her best to fill out the white bathing suit in *Creature Walks Among Us*.

The Gill Man behind bars but still the Gill Man! There was some effort to domesticate the Creature in *The Creature Walks Among Us* but as could have been predicted, he reverts to type in the end.

Our cast: That's Rex Reason as Dr. Thomas Morgan suiting up for some skin diving (and auditioning for the next Bond movie?) and Jeff Morrow as Dr. William Barton trying to talk Leigh Snowdon as wife Marcia Barton from going on the dangerous dive looking for the Gill Man. She doesn't listen.

The Deadly Mantis (1957)

What is it with the North Pole and fifties monsters? *The Thing, The Beast From 20,000 Fathoms*, and now this? Be that as it may, this lost gem follows the typical giant monster pattern as an oversized praying mantis is broken loose from the arctic ice, makes its way south (with the expected stopovers for mayhem), threatens Washington, D.C., and arrives in New York City only to be trapped in the Lincoln Tunnel and gassed to death by fearless members of the US military; hooray! Like *Them*, the makers of this film opt for an articulated puppet for the mantis instead of stop motion (or enlarged film of actual insects…brrrr) and largely succeed in showing it off in a number of impressive scenes. Genre regular William Hopper stars as the film's scientist with all the answers and Craig Stevens (what? Kenneth Tobey wasn't available?) plays the military attaché who, of course, gets the girl, in this case, wolf-bait Alix Talton.

Impressive matte shot of our cast in the foreground and rear screen projection of *The Deadly Mantis* puppet in the background.

That's William Hopper as Dr. Ned Jackson, Alix Talton as photographer Marge Blaine, and Craig Stevens as Col. Joe Parkman.

Alix Talton filled the role of professional woman Marge Blaine nicely… notwithstanding the attention she received from every male she encountered in *Deadly Mantis.*

William Hopper starred in a number of SF offerings before becoming a regular on the long running *Perry Mason* TV show.

Good combinations of puppet work and miniatures made the FX on *Deadly Mantis* as good as those used on *Them!* And the movie itself one of the little known genre gems of the 1950s

The Black Scorpion (1957)

For all of its stop motion effects, this film falls far short of expectations (FX were created by the great Willis O'Brien after all). Suffering from a plot that mimics *Them* far too closely, hampered by Mexican settings, and finally dragged down by an insufferable little kid who keeps getting in the way of the action, the film follows geologist Richard Denning (Dr. Hank Scott) as he investigates volcanic activity south of the border only to stumble across a nest of giant black scorpions. O'Brien does his best but the feature's low budget eventually betrays him with obvious model work and many FX shots repeated over and over again. But when silhouettes of the scorpions begin to appear instead of stop motion figures themselves, you know it's time to stick a fork in it. Even the presence of alluring Mara Corday as Theresa Alvarez and Denning's romantic interest can't raise the level of this snoozer beyond third tier status.

To be sure, many of the stop motion FX shots in *Black Scorpion* are impressive (such as this subterranean battle between a giant scorpion and spider) but they weren't enough to offset other liabilities such as animation shots using fewer frames per second and most especially the annoying presence of Mario Navarro as Juanito

The presence of Mara Corday went a long way toward keeping *The Black Scorpion* completely out of the fail category!

Richard Denning was a mainstay of 50s SF movies. He lucked out in *Black Scorpion* with lovely Mara Corday as his love interest!

Unfortunately, this unconvincing close up of the slavering jaws of a giant scorpion was used over and over again in *Black Scorpion*. But don't be put off; any stop motion work is better than no stop motion and more fun to watch than even Computer Generated Imagery (CGI)!

The Incredible Shrinking Man (1957)

Starring Grant Williams (among the pantheon of great 50s sci fi stars including Kenneth Tobey, Richard Carlson, Hugh Marlowe, William Hopper, Richard Denning, etc) and the luscious Randy Stuart (the radical transition from her form fitting attire seen at the start of the film to her bilious June Cleaver dresses in later scenes must have been intended to leave male viewers breathless), this top tier classic of the era tells the story of Scott Carey (Williams) as he passes through a strange cloud while at sea and then begins to shrink. Good direction by Jack Arnold, that master of 50s sci fi, at first intrigues then builds suspense quickly until Carey is trapped in his basement by a common house cat. From there, it's a struggle for survival as he continues to shrink and fights a climactic battle with a spider (maybe the same tarantula who starred in a previous Arnold film). Along with an evocative trumpet solo by Ray Anthony over the opening credits, the film also features wonderful FX and a script written by Richard Matheson, the author of the book that inspired it. In it, Matheson takes a completely opposite point of view from that of H. G. Wells in *Things to Come.* Here, no matter how Carey shrinks or what the life and death trials he must endure, the human spirit triumphs. The film concludes with Carey (even as he continues to shrink into nothingness) experiencing what amounts to a divine revelation: that all things, even the most insignificant, matter to God. Life indeed has a purpose beyond empty materialism or the pursuit of knowledge. ("To God, there is no zero!") A perfect example of what it takes for a film to be included among the top tier of SF films in this or any other era!

In the opening act of *Incredible Shrinking Man*, Grant Williams as Scott Carey, runs into a strange cloud that is never explained but likely some kind of radioactive fallout. Soon after, his life will change…forever!

Brief shots of Randy Stuart as Louise Carey at the start of *Incredible Shrinking Man* certainly helped viewers identify with her husband's later frustration and loss of self-esteem after he realizes that his shrinking was irreversible and that he would never be able to hold this bundle in his arms again!

Grant Williams as Scott Carey faces off against the spider in perhaps the most memorable sequence in *Incredible Shrinking Man*. What does it matter if a tarantula is unlikely to be found in a typical suburban basement?

The Monolith Monsters (1957)

The best of director Jack Arnold's "desert" films (he came up with the idea for this one while leaving the direction to John Sherwood). This time the story involves meteor fragments from space that grow as tall as skyscrapers threatening to overwhelm the entire planet before Grant Williams as geologist Dave Miller, manages to stop them by blowing up the local dam! Sherwood's directing grabs the viewer right from the start and never lets go as the fast paced plot moves things along. Special FX are by Clifford Stine who does an incredible job animating the alien monoliths giving them a convincing air of weight and size. One beautiful scene involves Williams and a fellow scientist as they brainstorm trying to figure out what makes the meteor fragments grow all while the answer is right outside as a thunderstorm sends sheets of rain against the windows! Featuring one of the most unique threats of any SF movie ever, *The Monolith Monsters* succeeds in evoking the sense of wonder that great science fiction is supposed to do.

This beautifully composed FX shot takes place near the end of *Monolith Monsters* as the stone objects are about to wipe out the tiny desert town of San Angelo.

Our cast: That's Les Tremane as newshound Martin Cochrane, Lola Albright as school teacher Cathy Barrett, Grant Williams as Dave Miller, and William Flaherty as police chief Dan Corey

Gant Williams and Lola Albright in a publicity shot for *Monolith Monsters*.

Jack Arnold, the man behind *Monolith Monsters*, *It Came from Outer Space*, *Tarantula*, *Incredible Shrinking Man*, and more. What other sci fi filmmaker could hold a candle to him?

Evocative scene in *Monolith Monsters* as Grant Williams' Dave Miller and Prof. Arthur Flanders played by Trevor Bardette try to figure out what makes the alien rocks grow as the answer is foreshadowed by a rainstorm just outside the lab window!

Kronos (1957)

Low budget but well done film that takes a good idea and runs with it. Astronomer Jeff Morrow discovers a mysterious object over the Earth that turns out to be an alien spacecraft on a mission to deposit a giant machine designed to drain all of Earth's energy and beam it back to its home planet. Good direction by Kurt Neuman of a story by Irving Block (who also worked on the special effects) delivers in style and atmosphere what it lacks in budget. Knowing their limitations, the producers restrain themselves and through judicious use of miniatures, mattes, stock footage, and composites manage to create one of the best of the lesser known SF films of the era. (That said, the best special effect in the movie remains attractive astro-photographer Barbara Lawrence in a white bathing suit!) The whole thing is topped off with some classy opening credits and music by Paul Sawtell and Bert Shefter.

Barbara Lawrence plays Jeff Morrows' co-worker and girlfriend in *Kronos*. *You* figure out why Morrows' character can barely notice her!

Impressive FX shot of Kronos device as it absorbs energy from a local power plant. With little money to work with and only a two week shooting sked, Jack Rabin, Irving Block, and Louis DeWitt really delivered for this low budget SF entry!

Another cool FX shot from *Kronos* this time showing the alien machine's innards. Those are our heroes looking down from where they landed atop the robot via helicopter!

That's Barbara Lawrence in the middle as Vera Hunter and Jeff Morrow on the right as Dr. Leslie Gaskell. The two are in a helicopter about to land on top of the Kronos device

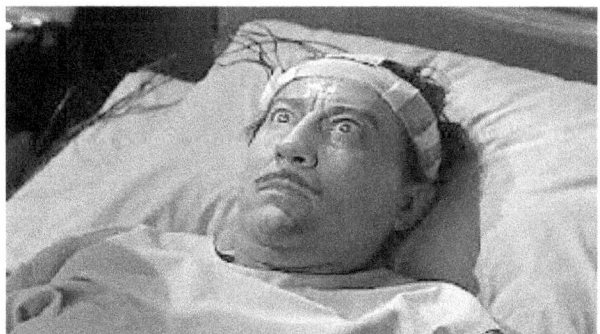

John Emery as the unlucky Dr. Hubbell Eliot undergoing shock therapy to try and shake him of alien possession. You got it! *Kronos* had a little of everything in its interesting plot.

20 Million Miles to Earth (1957)

A good plot involving a creature from Venus that grows at an alarming rate and ends up threatening modern day Rome. Generous amounts of Ray Harryhausen FX and strong opening scenes of downed rocket make this one of the select group of 50s simple but elegant SF classics. William Hopper as astronaut Robert Calder is okay but he's no substitute for Kenneth Tobey! Guess you can't have everything!

Once again, stop motion wizard Ray Harryhausen creates a monster that's not only startling in its design, but believable in the subtlety of its articulation such that when it's finally killed at the end of the movie, audiences can't help but feel sorry for it.

In an impressive opening sequence, Italian fishermen approach the downed Venus ship to rescue survivors. Harryhausen could handle standard FX as well as he could stop motion.

In a film loaded with FX action, this final scene with the Venusian creature just before being blasted from atop the Coliseum, still provided thrills as well as sympathy for an alien creature far from home.

Beautiful Joan Taylor provided thrills of a different kind as Marisa Leonardo, the film's romantic interest.

William Hopper as Astronaut Robert Calder was a semi-regular in 50s SF movies but his easy going style came in second to Kenneth Tobey's intensity.

The Quatermass Experiment (1955)

The UK's first meaningful entry into the cinematic SF sweepstakes was *The Quatermass Experiment* (or The *Creeping Unknown* as it was called in the US...which was the better title? You be the judge!) In it, the country's space program results in disaster when its first space rocket crashes into a farmer's field and the sole surviving astronaut transforms into a monster! The film started life as a TV serial written by Nigel Kneale before a fledgling Hammer Productions decided to turn it into a movie. Val Guest was hired to direct and American movie star Brian Donlevy cast as the no nonsense Prof. Bernard Quatermass. Guest takes a tight script and transforms it into a semi-noir film with an at times documentary feel to it as surviving astronaut Victor Carroon (scarily played by Richard Wordsworth) is slowly taken over and transformed into a shapeless, slimy monster! Wisely, FX are kept to a minimum with pieces of the creature coming to life in a lab grossly realistic. Donlevy provides the best Quatermass (there would ultimately be three movies in the series) who is not likeable at all in his single minded determination to explore space regardless of the cost either in money or human lives. A definite and refreshing departure from the square jawed hero scientists emerging in US cinema at the time. Heartily recommended!

Britain's first rocket into space returns in less than stellar style as emergency crews race to salvage the ship and rescue any surviving astronauts

Brian Donleby as Quatermass contemplates on what to do about creepy Victor Carroon played by Richard Wordswoth

Brian Donlevy as Quatermass examines a piece of the alien mass that broke out of its enclosure seeking to absorb some nearby lab animals.

Quatermass II (1957)

The second of the Quatermass films from Hammer studios (called *Enemy From Space* in the US) is the best of the three with stark b/w photography and direction by Val Guest who is also credited on the script along with Nigel Kneale who wrote the original BBC television serial. Both men keep the action moving along with American actor Brian Donlevy reprising his role as the humorless Prof. Quatermass. This time, he penetrates a secret government project that has been taken over by microscopic space creatures determined to transform the Earth's environment to one more suitable to their alien physiology. Again, FX are kept to a minimum with producers content with location shooting at an oil refinery and unfinished suburban development. The locations help to emphasize Guest's signature cinema verite style and an eerie but exciting score by James Bernard really sets a tone of growing paranoia. What special effects there are, are saved till the end when a pair of massive domes explode revealing alien creatures the size of small mountains! Probably the best SF film to come out of England hands down!

One of the giant domes featured in *Quatermass II* used as incubators to grow giant alien monsters!

Director Val Guest and star Brian Donlevy discuss a scene in Quatermass II

A disguised Brian Donlevy as Quatermass infiltrates the installation being used by the aliens to grow giant versions of themselves.

As big as a mountain, one of the alien giants breaks out from a shattered dome, threatening the world!

Monster That Challenged the World (1957)

In a plot similar to that of *Monolith Monsters* (not to mention any number of other giant insect, dinosaur on the loose movies), *The Monster That Challenged the World* (you gotta hand it to the filmmaker's PR department, they at least were earning their pay!) finds an army of giant mollusks (!) enervated by radiation, threatening to break loose from a lake and spread everywhere. The only hope is to stop them from escaping via a canal system that gives outlet to the sea. Can our heroes stop them in time? They will if director Arnold Laven, Tim Holt, and Audrey Dalton have anything to say about it. Well, maybe not Audrey Dalton who plays lab secretary Gail MacKenzie. Besides providing a romantic interest for Holt's Lt. Cmdr. John Twillinger, she also has a young daughter who manages to get them both trapped in a closet with a ravenous mollusk trying to break in. Hoo boy! Anyway, the suspense mounts until Twillinger rescues the two in the nick of time while preventing the monsters from breaking out of their inland lake. Whew! For a movie that doesn't have the advantage of Harryhausen's stop motion magic nor a budget worth mentioning, it's not bad. FX shots are kept to a minimum avoiding embarrassing situations for the producers and those that are used can at least pass muster. Meanwhile, relationships among the cast give audiences something to think about instead of the missing monsters. Not bad.

Audrey Dalton as Gail McKenzie confronts a world challenging monster as it threatens her daughter. The puppet work on the monster wasn't bad when it counted.

The FX crew prepare a giant mollusk for its close up

It's clear that Audrey Dalton's talents weren't fully exploited in *Monster That Challenged the World*!

Barbara Darrow as the rebellious Jody Simms is only on screen for a few minutes because she soon becomes food for a giant mollusk. Her mother warned her not to go near the beach!

Attack of the Crab Monsters (1957)

Okay, *Attack of the Crab Monsters* might not have had anything going for it but the title but so long as the producers stayed away from the actual giant crabs themselves, they were on reasonable solid ground. How could they not be with Russell Johnson in the cast? True, he didn't have much help but the concept of a handful of researchers stranded on an island infested by irradiataed, giant, malignant, personality absorbing, mind reading crabs did lend itself to a certain sense of isolation and paranoia. One of director Roger Corman's earliest efforts, he manages to create some suspense out of the doings particularly in a scene where the repetition of a strange sound turns out to be only the knocking of an object on the wall of a house. In another scene, a sailor falls out of a boat and when he's hauled back in, we find that he's somehow lost his head! Brrrr. For connoisseurs only.

Russell Johnson as electronics wiz Hank Chapman faces off with a giant crab at the climax of *Attack of the Crab Monsters*.

Early in the story, our team of researchers check out a cave entrance where strange sounds have been detected...

Pamela Duncan as Dr. Martha Hunter runs from a giant crab. Made for only $70,000 the crab itself was only scrap wood and paper mache and could only "move" when pulled by a couple of prop men

Because Pamela Duncan is a lot more interesting than paper mache giant crabs, here she is again, studying her lines for her next scene.

The Fly (1958)

Is it animal or vegetable? This classic entry can't decide whether it's a horror or science fiction movie. But whatever it is, it comes on strong with an opening sequence involving beautiful Patricia Owens (as Helene Delambre) caught at the controls of an industrial press after having just crushed her husband's head into a bloody mess. Interest continues to build until Owens tells the tale of husband David Hedison (as Andre Delambre) and his experiments in matter transferal. Here, the plot slows down somewhat before picking up again after Hedison's atoms get mixed up with a fly's. From there, things move more quickly ending at the point where the mystery began. Although the climactic scene involving the Hedison/fly thing about to be eaten by a spider is justly famous, it makes little sense on a logical level. Even so, the film was a hit for 20th Century Fox and spawned two sequels.

The disturbing climax to *The Fly*. That's Herbert Marshall as Inspector Charas and Vincent Price as Francois Delambre. If nothing else, *The Fly* boasted a good cast.

Beautiful Patricia Owens as Helene Delambre spiced up an otherwise slow moving central portion of *The Fly*!

When Al Hedison (Andre Delambre) appeared on TV, his name was David. Go figure.

Al Hedison as Andre Delambre (under the hood) informs wife Helene played by Patricia Owen that something has gone horribly wrong with his experiments…

Curse of the Demon (1958)

This one's a doozy! Director Jacques Tourneur (he of *Cat People* and *I Walked With a Zombie*) turns in a classy effort with this b-film due to his evocative and brilliant use of crisp, black and white cinematography. Turning on a clever twist in the plot, this is a first rate (if somewhat loose) adaptation of M.R.James' "Casting the Runes" about a convention on the supernatural where Dr. John Holden (played by Dana Andrews) is scheduled to debunk local demon worshipper Julian Carswell (played by Niall MacGinniss). Carswell sets out to prove the disbeliever wrong by siccing the demon of the title onto Holden. Among many notable scenes, the ones with Holden trespassing on Carswell's mist shrouded estate and his feeling of being followed in the narrow confines of a hotel corridor are particularly atmospheric. Oh, yeah! And the demon itself, towering over treetop level as it advances on its victims is impressive beyond what its costumy look might indicate. (Despite those scenes not having been shot by Tourneur who objected to showing the demon) And as if all that wasn't enough, the solid cast also includes attractive Peggy Cummins as Joanna Harrington! So what are you waiting for? Run, don't walk to see this filmic jewel!

Not exactly giving away the game since the demon is shown in the very first scene of *Curse of the Demon*, this shot shows how even a guy in a suit can be made to look cool under the proper cinematographic and costuming conditions!

One of the best scenes in *Curse of the Demon* as Dana Andrews, the disbelieving John Holden, is given his first taste of the supernatural. Use of foreshortening and optical effects help give this scene a sense of claustrophobic suspense.

Beautiful Peggy Cummins would knock 'em dead in any film she appeared in. It was just our luck that she was in so few!

It was only a question of which was creepier: the demon or Niall MacGinnis as a clown…

It! The Terror From Beyond Space (1958)

Okay, it has a low budget, an uninteresting cast, and horrible acting, but the plot is everything! (It was taken by scripter Jerome Bixby from A.E.Van Vogt's *Black Destroyer* after all). A bloodthirsty alien monster with more than human intelligence has stowed away aboard a rocket outbound from Mars and slowly forces the crew (headlined by B sci fi fave Marshall Thompson) up successive levels of the ship until they find themselves cornered in the capsule! (If it sounds familiar, it ought to; it's plot was in turn lifted by 1979's *Alien* which used the same ingenious ending). Keeping within their limited budget, the producers manage to create quite an elaborate set design that simulates the rocket's multiple levels (including fully installed ceilings) while delivering a compelling story. Still a fun film.

In a tense moment from *It!* The male members of the crew get ready to check out the engine room where a creature has stowed away. It sneaked aboard while the ship rested on the surface of Mars. Why in the world the mission was so heavily armed is a mystery.

Suspense mounts as a crew member crawls through access tunnels in search of the *It*!

Ray "Crash" Corrigan suited up as the monster in *It!* Overall, the creature design looked good and shots like this, obscured in smoke and fumes made it look even better!

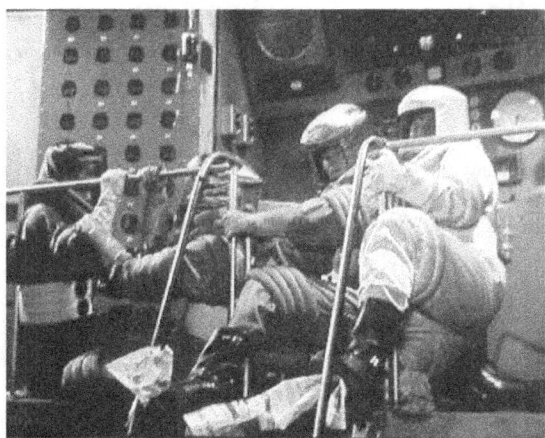

The heavily armed crew prepares for a last stand against *It!* The overall plot and final scene where the creature is sucked into space via an open airlock was lifted lock stock and barrel by a later film called *Alien*

Fiend Without a Face (1958)

This film definitely belongs among the bottom feeders but like all of the films noted in this volume it has at least some good qualities to recommend it not least of which is its sheer, hallucinatory nature! At an American military base in Canada, the natives are blaming atomic experiments for upsetting their livestock. Turns out that a local mad scientist has been experimenting with thought transference (or something) that has drawn creatures from another dimension which in turn feed on the radiation from the nearby atomic pile. Fair enough, but the aliens are nothing more than brains with spinal columns that they coil and use to spring onto their victims, choking them to death! No kidding! FX are pretty cool though, with stop motion used to animate the creatures and show how they dissolve into a disgusting mess. Nice b/w cinematography adds atmosphere in places and lots of stock footage of 1950s era military aircraft. Pretty Kim Parker (as Barbara Griselle acting opposite serious Marshall Thompson as Maj. Jeff Cummings) provides the film some needed accessories in particular, the quick shot of her wrapped only in a towel!

Group shot! A bunch of Fiends Without Faces gang up on a hapless citizen!

Kim Parker poses for a publicity shot. PR knew they had something with the pretty actress when they made her scene emerging from a shower the centerpiece of most of their advertising

Marshall Thompson and Kim Parker look out in horror at a gathering of hundreds of Fiends. By this point, they'd boarded themselves up in the office of mad scientist Prof. Walgate played by Kynaston Reeves. Expert management of the film's low budget paid dividends at the box office.

I Married a Monster From Outer Space (1958)

Don't be fooled by its title! This modest but entertaining film features attractive Gloria Talbott as the hapless newlywed whose husband is snatched virtually at the altar and replaced by a shape shifting alien…talk about sexual frustration! After a year of marriage and no sign of an impending pregnancy, Talbott finally decides that there's something not quite right with her husband. Following him one night, she discovers his true nature along with an alien spacecraft hidden in the woods. The film deals in a subject matter that, in a later era, could have been handled in a far more serious (and doubtless, more clinical) manner but manages nonetheless through suggestive dialogue and moody cinematography to convey the fearful strangeness of Talbott's situation as events slowly close in on her. For example, an unusually effective scene for 1950s SF includes aliens in the shape of police officers killing an unconscious man in cold blood and another disintegrating a prostitute for no good reason. Add to that some basic but effective FX and you have a recipe for a cool little thriller.

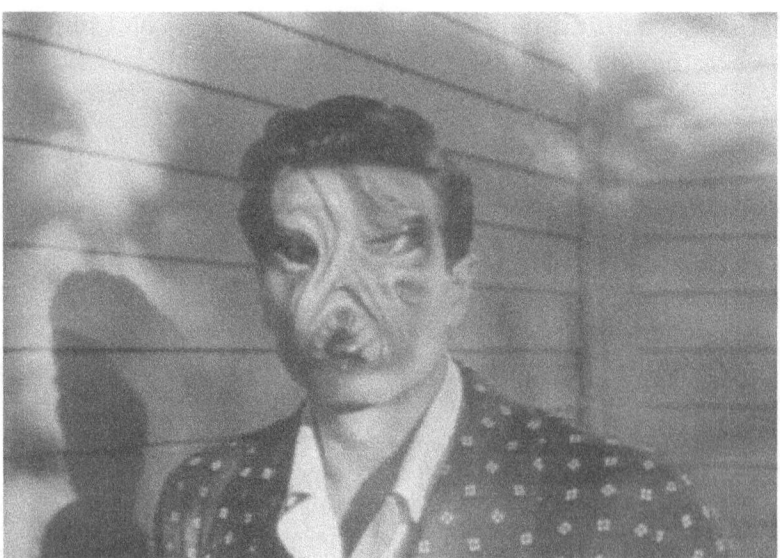

Tom Tryon's true nature as an alien is briefly revealed in this shot from *I Married a Monster*. But it wasn't the effects that marked the film, but rather its psycho-sexual subtext

Although what little FX there were in *I Married Monster* were serviceable, they really weren't the focus of the film

This shot of Gloria Talbot as Marge Farrell and Tom Tryon as Bill Farrell perfectly captures their dual roles as innocent but hopeful wife and scheming alien

The real husbands were kept in stasis aboard the aliens' spacecraft while their doppelgangers consorted with their wives!

Poor Tom Tryon's Bill Farrell missed his honeymoon with Gloria Talbot's Marge. Oh, the humanity!

The Space Children (1958)

After doing sterling service for any devotee of 50s science fiction cinema, director Jack Arnold had just completed his 1957 masterpiece *The Incredible Shrinking Man* when he lensed this late career entry. Unfortunately, something was lost in translation and due to money, casting, or script difficulties, or even loss of interest in the subject matter, *Space Children* lacked the smart, atmospheric tension of films such as *Monolith Monsters, It Came From Outer Space, Creature From the Lost Lagoon*, and *Tarantula*. The same lack of interest would also be felt in *Monster on the Campus*, another Arnold film of the 1950s. About a group of youngsters under the sway of a strange alien creature intent on preventing man from spreading his warlike ways into space, the film lacks real dramatic tension and strongly defined central characters. The children themselves (including a pre-*Rifleman* Johnny Crawford and Sandy Descher who played the little girl who cried "Them!") are pretty limited in their acting abilities. It's night time beach locations do capture some of the old Arnold eeriness though. A rarely seen, hard to find film that nonetheless ends in 50s fashion quoting from St. Matthew. Overall, still an entertaining entry in the era's SF pantheon. And don't miss Russell Johnson in a brief role, the sole victim of the alien menace!

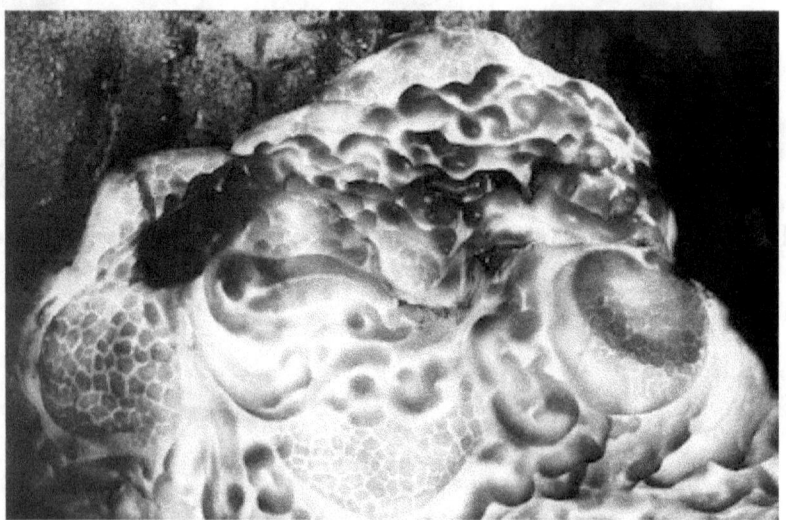

The amorphous alien creature from *Space Children*. FX were at a premium for this cheapie.

The children of *Space Children*. That's Sandy Descher of *Them!* fame third from left.

With the aid of the alien creature, the *Space Children* sneak past guards onto a missile site to sabotage an atomic bomb test.

In happier days. The family Brewster as they arrive for dad's new job on a top security missile base. Mom doesn't look too happy with the prospect!

The Crawling Eye (1958)

The Crawling Eye nee "The Trollenberg Terror," was another British SF entry of the 1950s fronted by American actor Forest Tucker as UN science agent Alan Brooks. Seems scientists somewhere in the Swiss town of Trollenberg have a problem: a stationary radioactive cloud has appeared on a nearby mountaintop. Can Brooks do anything about it? Meanwhile, Brooks has arrived in town on a train that also carries Anne and Sarah Pilgrim (played by Janet Munro and Jennifer Jayne respectively). The sister act just happens to include a mind reading routine that turns out to be the real thing when Anne begins to read messages involving the radioactive cloud which turns out to be hiding an alien invasion. For most of the film, producers wisely concentrate on characterization and atmosphere which works well. When the aliens make their appearance of the movie's climax, we understand why. A combination of miniatures and puppetry, the aliens, that look like giant crawling eyes natch, are more or less unconvincing with the exception of one shot of one filling up the door space of the hotel set. Very weird! While definitely a lesser light among 50s SF movies, *The Crawling Eye* is still quite enjoyable while boasting not one, but two attractive female leads who go a long way to making the FX-less moments in this picture a lot easier to take.

Pretty Janet Munro played clairvoyant Anne Pilgrim in *The Crawling Eye*.

...and Jennifer Jayne as sister Sarah Pilgrim isn't hard on the eyes either!

One of the aliens in the form of a single, huge eye fills a doorway in this iconic shot from *The Crawling Eye*!

Forrest Tucker as Alan Brooks peers over a newspaper as he considers the Pilgrim sisters sitting across from him. Is he wondering about their mind reading act or deciding which one to ask for a date?

First Man Into Space (1959)

Extremely low budget epic from the folks who brought you *Fiend Without a Face*. Marshall Thompson returns as Commander Charles Prescott whose reckless brother is slated to be *The First Man Into Space*. Unfortunately, his flight runs into trouble and crashes back to Earth. The brother, played by Bill Edwards, finds himself coated with "cosmic dust," nature's way of protecting objects traveling through the ether. Back on earth, however, unable to speak and stumbling around half blind, our astronaut cannot be anything but a monster right? Surprise! Ending is both touching and tragic. Not bad. Our pal Marshall Thompson is good, helping keep the film grounded in nourish reality while co-star Marla Landi provides the proper degree of emotion.

The climactic scene in *First Man Into Space*. With only a single eye visible, Bill Edwards as the unfortunate Dan Prescott, manages to convey heartrending emotion as, knowing he is to die, bids goodbye to girlfriend Tia Francesca played by Marla Landi. That's Marshall Thompson with the oxygen mask, by the way.

A serious Marshall Thompson contemplates the fate of his brother, astronaut Dan Prescott

Beautiful Mara Landi played the unfortunate girlfriend of *The First Man Into Space*. But would brother Marshall Thompson be there to help pick up the pieces? Soap opera? Sure. But it was human interest sub-currents in 50s SF that set it apart from many post *Star Wars* films that tended to blur the line between men and women.

Journey to the Center of the Earth (1959)

Lost cities? Check! Giant lizards? Check! Weird, otherworldly landscapes? Check! Exploding volcanoes? Check! The hollow Earth? Check! You name it, this one's got it…well, maybe except for space ships, but otherwise, this period film set in the early days of the sometimes cutthroat age of exploration and archeology definitely keeps the viewer watching even though the FX are sketchy at times (any movie whose very first shots includes stock footage and process work wouldn't seem very promising to the discerning viewer) but held together by Bernard Herman's atmospheric score and some really good sets and matte shots (those featuring the aforementioned giant lizards and the human actors were impressively seamless) this movie makes for a fast moving 132 minutes!

Our team of intrepid spelunkers…Victorian style! That's Peter Ronson as Hans Bjelke, Pat Boone as Alec McEwan, Arlene Dahl as Carla Goteborg, and James Mason as Sir Oliver Lindenbrook.

Nice combination of effects with lizard style "dinosaurs" on left, foreground stalactites, and actual film of our spelunkers dragging a raft to the subterranean ocean on right.

James Mason and Arlene Dahl admire the giant mushroom set for Journey to the Center of the Earth.

Return of the Fly (1959)

A plodding affair with little in the way of atmosphere involves Brett Halsey, the inventor's son from the first film now all grown up and wanting to follow in his father's footsteps despite the wishes of uncle Vincent Price. A lab assistant scheming to steal the secret of the matter transfer machine and sell it to the highest bidder is the instrument that manages to get Halsey into the machine along with a fly to reproduce the same results as in the original film: namely giving Halsey the head and arm of a fly. Mayhem ensues and not even set decoration Danielle De Metz is enough to recommend this turkey.

Ugh! The less said the better!

Vincent Price reprised his role from the first *Fly* movie and launched the second half of his career through the 1960s as a horror movie icon

Danielle de Metz as Cecile Bonnard was mostly set decoration in *Return of the Fly* but was likely the only ray of light in a mostly dreary entry

Brett Halsey as Philippe Delambre as the Fly puts the squeeze on Danielle de Metz as Cecile Bonnard. *Now* he's interested?

The Time Machine (1960)

Part of a trend that saw adaptations of novels by Jules Verne and H.G.Wells done as period pieces with this film taking place in 1900. Unfortunately, casting, production values, and overall lackadaisical pace by director George Pal doom this entry to being a mostly dull affair. However, a couple scenes do manage to suggest some of the wonder presented in the original novel...

One of the cooler FX shots in *The Time Machine* as Rod Taylor aka H.G. Wells, arrives in the far future.

Rod Taylor as H.G. Wells prepares to hop aboard his time machine.

Yvette Mimieux starred as future nymph Weena in *The Time Machine*.

Production photo of Yvette Mimieux in costume as Weena

Rod Taylor lacked charisma as the lead in *The Time Machine*. But then, H.G. Wells wasn't exactly Mr. Excitement himself.

Village of the Damned (1960)

The first 15 minutes of this film has one of the best opening hooks ever done (maybe even better than the opening scenes of *The Thing* which take a bit longer to develop) and if this movie isn't a faithful adaptation of the novel by John Wyndham, it ought to be! The film suggests that a plot involving the impregnation of every fertile woman in a quiet English village is one of alien invasion but it's never spelled out. The strange looking, silver haired offspring develop rapidly and before you know it, they're threatening the world! Adapted by Stirling Siliphant from Wyndham's novel, *The Midwich Cuckoos*, the film features well paced direction by Wolf Rilla (who he?) who manages to keep the viewer interested all the way through. The star however, an aging George Sanders as Prof. Gordon Zellaby, is too old for lovely Barbara Shelley who plays his wife Anthea and mother to one of the alien children. Overall, a wonderful example of the kind of fantastic filmmaking that once came out of England which today seems satisfied merely to offer American film companies studio space.

The kreepy kids of *Village of the Damned*. The glowing eyes were ordered removed for British release.

From the intriguing opening scenes of *Village of the Damned*. A kind of invisible force field is thrown around Midwich. Anyone crossing its boundaries falls immediately unconscious.

Lovely Barbara Shelley as Anthea Zellaby was too youthful and vivacious for aging star George Sanders in *Village of the Damned*.

George Sanders as Prof. Gordon Zellaby was too old for the part; that, and the fact that his heart just didn't seem to be in the role.

House of Usher (1960)

The first of eight films in director Roger Corman's successful series of adaptations of stories by writer Edgar Allan Poe. But as fine an adaptation as *House of Usher* is ("The Fall of..." was left off the title for some obscure reason), it's marred by having a similar plot to the director's *Pit and the Pendulum* lensed the next year ie young man arrives at spooky mansion owned by barely sane Vincent Price to find out about a young woman living there (in this case it's a girlfriend, in *Pit* it was a sister). That said, the usual sumptious sets and a script written by Richard Matheson keep the viewer's attention and move the story along. Vincent Price as Roderick Usher chews the scenery, Mark Damon is suitably intense as Philip Winthrop, the betrothed of Madeline Usher played by Myrna Fahey.

One of the hallmarks of Corman's Poe adaptations is the picture gallery. In contrast to the period settings of the films, paintings of deceased family members or former masters of the house were invariably done in modern or expressionistic styles. Here, Vincent Price as Roderick Usher gives Philip Winthrop, played by Matt Damon, a tour of his mad ancestors.

Atmospheric set featuring the House of Usher. Another feature of Corman's Poe films was the establishing matte shot of some spooky mansion or castle shown at the beginning of each film.

Myrna Fahey played Madeline Usher, who plots to drive her brother mad…to her regret!

Vincent Price as Roderick Usher gave a wonderfully hammy performance that paradoxically, was convincing as the disturbed, distraught, and ultimately mad, master of the *House of Usher*.

Day the Earth Caught Fire (1961)

Surprisingly well done film about atomic testing that sets the Earth on a collision course with the sun! Makers sensibly keep things within the limits of a low budget while convincing viewers that Earth's temperatures continue to rise to intolerable limits. Continues tradition of British fixation on end of world scenarios that was most prevalent in its SF literature. Unlike American films of the time, this movie's protagonist played by a cynical Edward Judd (as reporter Peter Stenning) is an anti-hero more obviously and obnoxiously interested in bedding his leading lady (Janet Munro as Jeannie Craig) than treating her with respect. Produced and directed by Val Guest, the story never falters, capturing the viewer's attention from the start with a realistic depiction of a big city newsroom and continuing on right to the end. Arthur Christianson, a former editor for the *Daily Express*, gives a star turn as Jeff Jefferson, the editor of the paper covering the end of the world story. Watching the scenes with him in action behind the big desk is worth the price of admission! Although the film's cynical, even hopeless message seems to hold at the conclusion, a final shot of a church steeple with the sound of bells tolling suggests a happy ending after all. Recommended!

London swathed in fog. *Day the Earth Caught Fire* **begins with a series of arresting images including this event that allows people on the street to see only a few feet in front of them.**

Judicious use of matte shots like this showing a dried up River Thames went a long way to making the vents of *Day the Earth Caught Fire* **convincing.**

Cynical, obnoxious, unethical, and an all around creep where Janet Munro's Jeannie Craig is concerned, Edward Judd as Peter Stenning is a different kind of SF protagonist. No need to wonder why his character was also divorced!

Janet Munro as telephone operator Jeannie Craig, was the unfortunate target of Stennis' attentions. Okay, he may have had good reasons for it, but did he have to be so obnoxious about it?

The editorial conference scenes in *Day the Earth Caught Fire* are some of the film's best due mainly to the performance of Arthur Christianson as editor Jeff Jefferson (second from left)

Voyage to the Bottom of the Sea (1961)

Noble attempt by producer/director Irwin Allen to tell the tale of a super submarine as it battles its way through various dangers from giant octopi and old mine fields to mutiny and sabotage in order to launch a nuclear missile into the atmosphere and prevent the Earth from burning up from an enflamed Van Allen belt. Unfortunately, although staffed with a supporting cast of yesteryear's movie stars (Walter Pigeon, Peter Lorre, and Joan Fontaine), elaborate sets, and passable FX, and early appearances by beautiful Barbara Eden and sinister Michael Ansara, none are enough to save the plodding story or its unlikely premise. And talk about getting off on the wrong foot; the film's introductory credits are backed up by a cloying title song as performed by Frankie Avalon (who also co-stars) more suitable to a Tammy or Gidget entry. That said, the movie was a hit at the time leading to a successful TV series and clearly influencing the Star Trek franchise.

The two female leads of *Voyage to the Bottom of the Sea*: Barbara Eden as Lt. Cathy Connors and Joan Fontaine as Dr. Susan Hiller.

The real star of *Voyage to the Bottom of the Sea*. The *Seaview* breaks surface in a dramatic scene from the movie. FX that made the super submarine look as real as possible on screen were crucial in making the film's story believable.

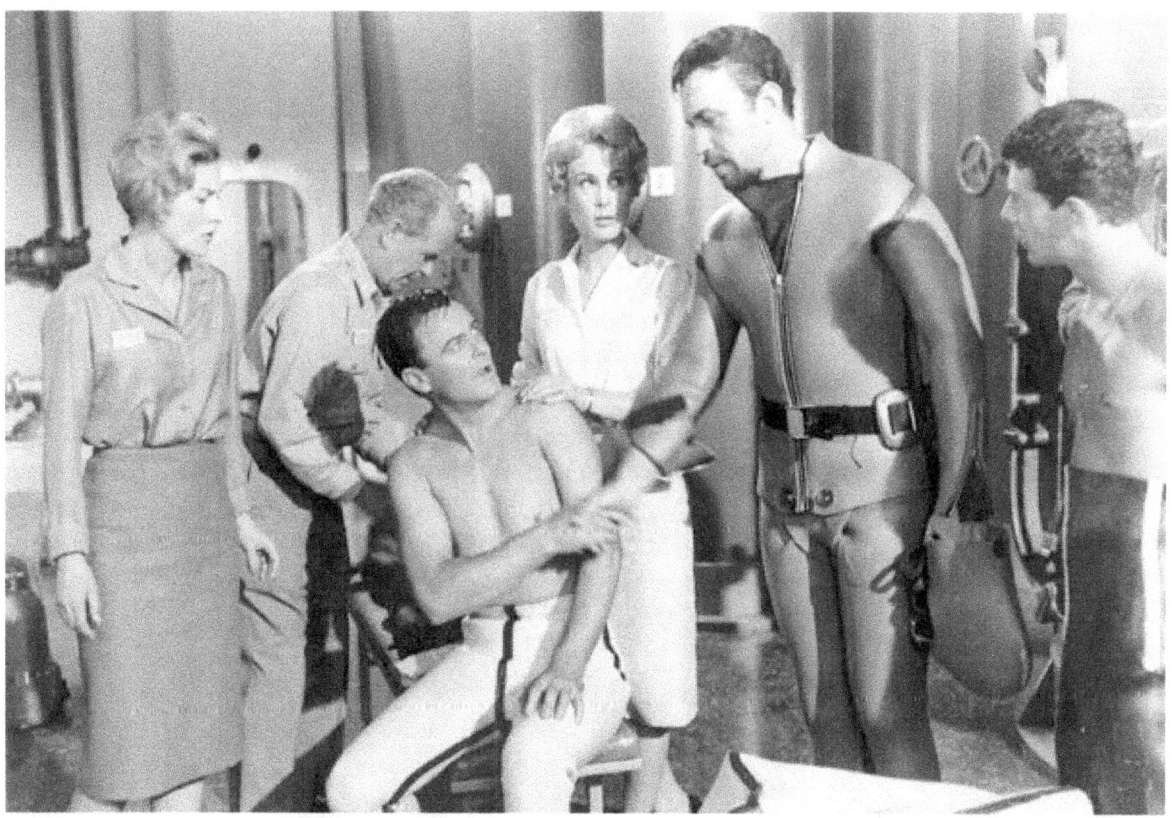

Because you have to have at least one scuba diving scene in a movie called *Voyage to the Bottom of the Sea*! Joan Fontaine on the right, Regis Toomey as Dr. Jamieson next, Robert Sterling as Capt. Lee Crane sitting, Barbara Eden, and fan fave Michael Ansara as Miguel Alvarez (who was married to Eden at the time).

The Innocents (1961)

Atmospheric adaptation of Henry James' classic story *The Turn of the Screw* leaves the viewer with the question: was there an evil force in the big, old house in the English countryside or was it all in the tutor's mind? Otherwise nicely directed in crisp black and white by Jack Clayton (the setting of an isolated country estate with its brooding towers, shadowy corridors, and elaborate gardens is made to order for a ghost story) who builds good mood and atmosphere. The two children played by Martin Stephens and a quite young Pamela Franklin are perfectly cast as children who may or may not know what is really going on.

Is it real or all in her head? In this scene at least, it looks literal with the ghost of the evil valet (Peter Quint played by Peter Wyngard) hovering behind little Miles (played by Martin Stephens)

Creepy scene from *The Innocents* as specter of Miss Jessel appears across a pond.

Do Martin Stephens and Pamela Franklin as brother and sister Miles and Flora seem Innocent to you?

Deberah Kerr as governess Miss Giddens descends the stairs in one of many atmospheric scenes in *The Innocents*.

The Pit and the Pendulum (1961)

Roger Corman directs this entry in his justly celebrated series of loose Poe adaptations this time with a dandy script by SF and horror author Richard Matheson. Once again, Vincent Price is teetering on the edge of madness as a young man played by John Kerr stops by the gloomy Spanish castle to inquire about his sister (the gorgeous opening matte shot of Price's castle alone is worth the price of admission!). However, the visitor soon finds himself entangled in mounting mystery and an adulterous love affair whose purpose is to drive Price out of his mind. It works, with the only ray of light being attractive Luana Anders who manages to save Kerr from falling victim to a raving Price and his see sawing pendulum of death! Great stuff that hasn't aged at all over the last fifty years!

Opening matte shot for *Pit and the Pendulum*.

Ka chink! Climactic scene from *Pit and the Pendulum* as Vincent Price as Nicholas Medina bids adieu to John Kerr as Francis Barnard.

Vincent Price as Nicholas Medina goes mad and strangles Barbara Steele who plays his conniving wife Elizabeth.

Luanda Anders played Catherine Medina, Nicholas' sister and was the saving grace in *Pit and the Pendulum*.

Luana Anders as Elizabeth and John Kerr as Francis Barnard

Mysterious Island (1961)

Not quite faithful adaptation of the Jules Verne novel nevertheless has everything that the team of Ray Harryhausen and producer Charles H. Schneer can throw into it: Civil War action, sunken cities, pirates, Captain Nemo and the *Nautilus*, oversized sea monsters, crabs, ostriches, and bees, all of it considerably enhanced by the presence of leggy Beth Rogan in a very un-Victorian mini skirt! Action packed story never lets up thanks to fine direction by Cy Enfield while Bernard Hermann provides the most exciting score of his career. Top notch FX including a number of gorgeous matte shots are pure eye candy making this one of the best fantasy/sci fi entries of the period.

One of a number of spectacular matte shots from *Mysterious Island*.

Our castaways battle a giant crab courtesy of Ray Harryhausen!

Gorgeous Beth Rogan in her decidedly un-Victorian mini outfit was a special effect that needed no enhancement!

The dramatic possibilities of stop motion was demonstrated in this scene when Michael Callan as Herbert Brown and Beth Rogan as Elinor Fairchild were shown standing in front of the cave entrance. Hearing the buzz of an insect, they duck inside and a few seconds later, when the bee lands at the entrance, its sudden appearance seemingly in the same shot that the two actors have just left is jarring to the viewer and demonstrates the size of the bee as well as its potential menace.

Burn, Witch, Burn! (1962)

Burn, Witch, Burn or as it was known in the UK, "Night of the Eagle," was based on the Fritz Leiber novel Conjure Wife. Leiber was lucky too, in having fellow weird/SF writers Richard Matheson and Charles Beaumont collaborating on the script and determined to do the book justice. And they do too for this low budget affair starring Peter Wyngarde as college professor Norman Taylor and Janet Blair as wife Tansy. Although Leiber's original concept of women secretly practicing witchcraft to aid themselves and their unsuspecting men is a good one, the college campus setting and its administrative political scene makes for an unexciting setting. But Matheson and Beaumont as well as director Sidney Hayers do their best to keep things lively including having a stone eagle come to life and attack Taylor. It's fun to see the agnostic Taylor destroy all of his wife's supernatural safeguards against attacks by other witches and then begin to suffer one mishap after another. A forgotten little classic.

Peter Wyngarde as Prof. Norman Taylor expresses his belief in rationalism over superstition. Everything he believes in will be tested over the course of *Burn, Witch, Burn*!

Janet Blair as Tansy, is dismayed to find that her husband has discovered her secret and destroyed all of her protective charms.

Fun scene where women working witchcraft to promote their men talk in innuendo that goes completely over the head of the blissfully ignorant male. The expressions on their faces and body language tell you all you need to know about their intentions regarding breaking past Tansy's own protective magic!

With her protective spells gone, Tansy becomes prey to scheming rivals who urge her to self destruction…

In a climactic scene, Norman Taylor confronts Flora Carr (Margaret Johnson), the main witch behind all that has been happening to him since he destroyed his wife's protections.

Panic in Year Zero (1962)

Hollywood legend Ray Milland both starred in and directed this low budget but surprisingly taut post atomic disaster thriller. It begins unassumingly enough as mild mannered Milland takes his family camping in the mountains but soon devolves into a desperate race with panicky hordes fleeing an irradiated Los Angeles. Early in the picture, as the family reaches higher altitudes, they look back toward the distant city only to see a giant mushroom cloud rising over it. Chilling and quite effective! Also, a nice touch is Milland's wife as she watches the man she thought she knew become a grim survivalist bent on keeping his family alive no matter what.

The typical American family looks back as Los Angeles goes up in an atomic cloud. That's Jean Hagen as Ann Baldwin on the left, Ray Milland as Harry Baldwin, Frankie Avalon as son Rick, and Mary Mitchel as daughter, Karen.

Reverse angle. This was the only FX shot in the entire film; but it didn't need any more as good drama and interesting situations was all that was needed to keep *Panic in Year Zero* moving forward.

Law and order break down. Without the use of over the top violence, *Panic in Year Zero* manages to create a sense of unease as society falls apart and it's every man for himself. Here the Baldwin family is stopped by local vigilantes keeping strangers out of their town.

After daughter Karen is raped by renegade toughs, her father and brother, with no law available but their own, track them down and kill them

Father Baldwin gives son Rick a lecture on the use of firearms…and the new facts of life!

Carnival of Souls (1962)

Bargain basement cheapie that makes up for lack of nearly everything with plenty of atmosphere and an abandoned dance pavilion set amid the salt flats of a receding lake in Utah. It was the chance discovery of the ruined pavilion that inspired director Herk Harvey to make the film (based on the classic *Twilight Zone* episode "The Hitchhiker" that was in turn an adaptation of a radio play) on time off from his regular job producing films for local industry. Like the previous versions, Mary Henry, played by Candace Hilligoss, is killed in a car accident but doesn't know it. She spends the rest of the movie having out of body experiences and dodging the unwanted attentions of local pervert and next door tenant John Linden played with appropriate sleaze by Sidney Berger before finally being overcome by a bunch of dancing corpses at the weird dance hall. Whew!

Candace Hilligoss as Mary Henry is apparently the only survivor after the car she was riding in plunges from a bridge.

The abandoned dance hall that inspired Herk Harvey to produce *Carnival of Souls*.

Friendly neighborhood stalker John Linden played by Sidney Berger puts the moves on Candace Hilligoss

Climactic "carnival" scene wherein Mary Henry observes dead people tripping the light fantastic. Will she join them?

Jason and the Argonauts (1963)

First and best of FX great Ray Harryhausen's fantasy epics can be dull in places (somewhat wooden performances by Todd Armstrong in the lead and Nancy Kovach as Medea are offset by fun-loving Hercules played against type by the wonderful Nigel Green) but elaborate sets and fabulous stop motion effects more than make up for it! Adding to the pleasure is a moody score by Bernard Herrmann which opens with a jarring clash of cymbals in the opening credits followed by a blast of horns that set the stage for mythic doings by the crew of the *Argo* including battles with the giant Talos, annoying harpies, the many-headed Hydra, and of course, the film's signature sequence featuring an army of animated skeletons! Great stuff!

Climactic skeleton fight scene in *Jason and the Argonauts* is justifiably famous not only for its visual dazzle but as an example of an FX artist at the peak of his craft. It will likely stand as Ray Harryhausen's most well known achievement.

...and who could forget Talos, the other Harryhausen signature effect sequence in *Jason and the Argonauts?* Not us!

Sorry Ray! Your FX wizardry had nothing to do with Nancy Kovack as the mysterious Medea. She was a special effect all on her own!

Day of the Triffids (1963)

Well paced adaptation of the novel by John Wyndham in which strange lights in the sky not only render everyone on earth but a few lucky people blind, but also bring spores that grow into giant, mobile plants hungry for human flesh! The film is better than it sounds as it follows parallel plot threads, one of a few sighted survivors (among them Howard Keel as land bound sailor Bill Masen, Nicole Maurey as Christine Durant, and Janina Faye as schoolgirl Susan who gather into a makeshift family) as they make their way across a devastated Europe ravaged by lawless gangs and hordes of triffids and a couple waging their own lonely battle trapped in an isolated lighthouse. Good direction by Steve Sekely although the plot doesn't follow the book exactly. Which might be for the better. Like the *Quatermass* films, *Triffids* had its genesis from a BBC television serial. FX are basic but serviceable and though slow moving triffids don't seem very formidable in the beginning, they…dare I say it? Grow on you by the end of the film. As in many SF films of this period, the story ends on a hopeful note as Earth's survivors are seen streaming into a church in thanksgiving.

Day of the Triffids' **makeshift family: Howard Keel as Bill Masen, Janina Faye as Susan, and Nicole Maurey as Christine Durant**

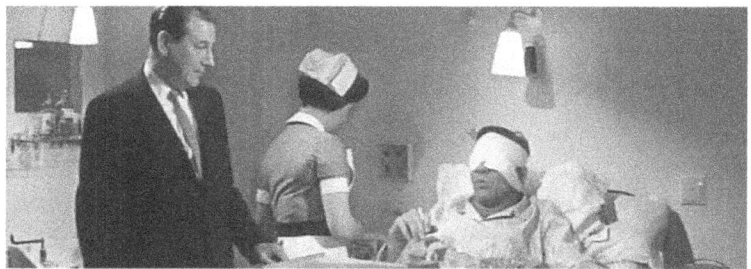

Howard Keel misses the fateful meteor shower due to eye surgery.

Howard Keel as Bill Masen holds back the Triffid horde with a jury rigged blow torch.

Day of the Triffids **was adorned with not one but two attractive leads. Here's the lovely Janette Scott who played Karen Goodwin trapped in a lighthouse besieged by Triffids with husband Tom Goodwin played by Kierwin Moore. The other lead was Nicole Maury who played Christine Durant.**

The Haunted Palace (1963)

Director Roger Corman teams up again with scripter Charles Beaumont to adapt (very loosely!) H.P. Lovecraft's story "The Strange Case of Charles Dexter Ward" with a veneer of Edgar Allen Poe to make it palatable to Corman's investors. Be that as it may, as an early Lovecraft film adaptation, it does name drop such references as Yog Sothoth, Cthulhu, and the Necronomicon possibly for the first time on the big screen…nothing to sneeze at! Nice matte shot of Vincent Price's spooky castle makes up a little for the rather limited village set where deformed humans hang out in dark alleys and locked attic rooms. Fun.

Debra Paget as Ann Ward is introduced to her betrothed…Yog Sothoth!

She doesn't seem too happy about it!

Another nice matte shot of a spooky mansion, this time for *The Haunted Palace*.

The Haunted Palace has the distinction of being one of the first if not *the* first movies to make specific mention of elements from H.P. Lovecraft's Cthulhu Mythos. Here we see the cover of the fabled *Necronomicon*. Wonder if the prop book was covered in human skin like the original?

One of the unfortunate inhabitants of Arkham. Cursed by sorcery emanating from *The Haunted Palace*!

The Haunting (1963)

This intensely atmospheric adaptation of Shirley Jackson's novel *The Haunting of Hill House* comes courtesy of director Robert Wise, cinematographer Davis Boulton, and score by Humphrey Searle. Together with the film's cast of characters who must endure an extended stay in the "house that was born bad," they explore the question of whether it's really ghosts that haunt Hill House or figments of the human mind. Or is it the psychic powers of the troubled Julie Harris as Evelyn Lance run amok? The brooding pile of Hill House that dominates the film's visual landscape isn't telling.

The spooky pile that stood in for Hill House was actually Eddington Park in Warwickshire, England.

Our cast: Claire Bloom as Theodora, Russ Tamblyn as Luke Sanderson, Julie Harris as Eleanor Lance, and Richard Johnson as Dr. John Markway.

Is it a face or isn't it? *The Haunting* **was one of the first films to explore the psychological side of horror.**

Clearly, Claire Bloom and Julie Harris believe it's real!

One of the scariest moments in *The Haunting* takes place in Julie Harris' bedroom. There, as she and Claire Boom huddle together, sounds of heavy footfalls followed by sudden bangings against the door make them and audiences jump. If that weren't enough, when the noise stops, the door begins to bulge inward threatening to break down letting in whatever is on the other side…

First Men in the Moon (1964)

Nigel Kneale, script writer of the successful *Quatermass* serials broadcast on BBC television and later adapted into a successful series of films, teams up with the Charles H. Schneer company that included Ray Harryhausen as its chief FX wizard, to produce *First Men in the Moon*, another period adaptation of an H.G. Wells novel. Cast as Arnold Bedford, Edward Judd again plays a somewhat ne'er do well writer who manages to keep girlfriend Katherine Callendar played by Martha Hyer on a string. They fall in with Prof. Joseph Cavor played with nutty aplomb by Lionel Jeffries who has invented an anti-gravity substance which he uses to paint a hollow metal ball that he proposes to fly to the Moon. Taking Arnold with him (and Katherine as a stowaway), the mission is a success! The ball crashes and rolls onto the Moon's barren surface and as the humans begin to explore, they discover a Lunar civilization of insectoids called Selenites as well as plethora of fun Harryhausen creatures. The film, directed by Nathan Juran, is slow in getting started but once on the Moon, it's one visual marvel after another. The movie is also enhanced by a prologue and epilogue in which modern UN space officials visit an elderly Arnold in a British nursing home who proves to them that their recently successful mission to the Moon wasn't history's first!

Prof. Cavor's "spaceship" comes to a rest on the surface of the Moon.

Surprised astronauts discover that they may not be the "First Men in the Moon!"

Lovely Martha Hyer en dishabillier in a publicity shot for *First Men in the Moon*. She could've done better than Edward Judd's Arnold Bedford!

Lionel Jeffries plays the apparently erratic Prof. Cavor.

A group of delightful Harryhausen animated Selenites confer on the fate of our fearless Moon explorers!

Masque of the Red Death (1964)

Classy, low budget Roger Corman directed and Charles Beaumont scripted adaptation of Edgar Allen Poe's story of the same name with genuine moments of downright strangeness; even has a metaphorical, symbolic sub-text (borrowed from the best source too, Ingmar Bergman's *Seventh Seal*)! Jane Asher is cute.

The personification of pestilence, in this case, the Red Death, is symbolically represented as playing cards with a little girl, the last survivor of her village. Will she live or will she die?

Vincent Price as Prince Prospero confronts a disguised Red Death during the dance macabre sequence.

Jane Asher as Francesca was a considerable asset to *Masque of the Red Death*!

Recognizing her beauty beneath grime and dirt, Prospero takes Francesca, played by Jane Asher, from her village where plague has broken out. Seeing her concern for her father and fiancé, he takes them as well, intending to use them for the satisfaction of his sadistic lusts.

Prospero invites his guests to enjoy themselves within the safety of his castle even as the peasants outside die of the plague.

Robinson Crusoe on Mars (1964)

If the theme of this movie were pitched today, H-wood types would call it a "high concept," a unique idea that can be summed up in a few words. In this case, remake Daniel Defoe's classic novel as a science fiction story with the Crusoe character stranded on Mars instead of a desert island. Sure! But despite adequate FX, desert settings, and nice direction by veteran Byron Haskin, it's clear the film would have been much better off if the modern Crusoe had been stranded on a planet outside our solar system. In the mid-1960s enough was known about Mars, even by the general public, to make the elements presented here fanciful to say the least. Still, it holds up pretty well as a story of faith, trust, friendship, and survival; things not readily found in more cynical SF films of a later era.

Its desert locations, like they did for many of Jack Arnold's SF films of the 50s, worked well in establishing a believable setting for Mars in *Robinson Crusoe on Mars*.

Paul Mantee as astronaut Christopher Draper had sufficient charisma to carry most of *Robinson Crusoe on Mars* by himself.

Victor Lundin played Friday, an alien slave freed by Draper. Lundin also has the distinction of having composed a song based on the movie. Don't laugh! It isn't half bad!

Model work was acceptable early in *Robinson Crusoe on Mars*.

A pre-Batman Adam West as command module pilot Col. Dan McReady filled out the limited cast of *Robinson Crusoe on Mars*.

The Time Travelers (1964)

This quirky film isn't on our list simply because it involves time travel (it's said to have been the inspiration for Irwin Allen's *Time Tunnel* TV show), but because it's also a showcase for a number of SF concepts including space travel, mutants, an apocalyptic future, and robots! Admittedly director Ib Melchior has his moments of humor (particularly those involving Steve Franken's wide eyed engineer as he tours the last humans' future refuge and attempts to pick up the far more sexually sophisticated femmes who live there), but overall, the film presents its subject seriously and even displays a touch of humanity as Merry Anders' scientist brings a certain amount of sympathy to the wretched mutants whom the normal humans fear and disdain. A fun film of the far distant year of 2071 that deserves at least a little more notice than it has. Be on the lookout for Forest J. Ackerman, so-called professional science fiction fan, who makes a short appearance! Also beware a similar film *World Without End* (1956) that has the same premise but approaches the issues involved in a less realistic way.

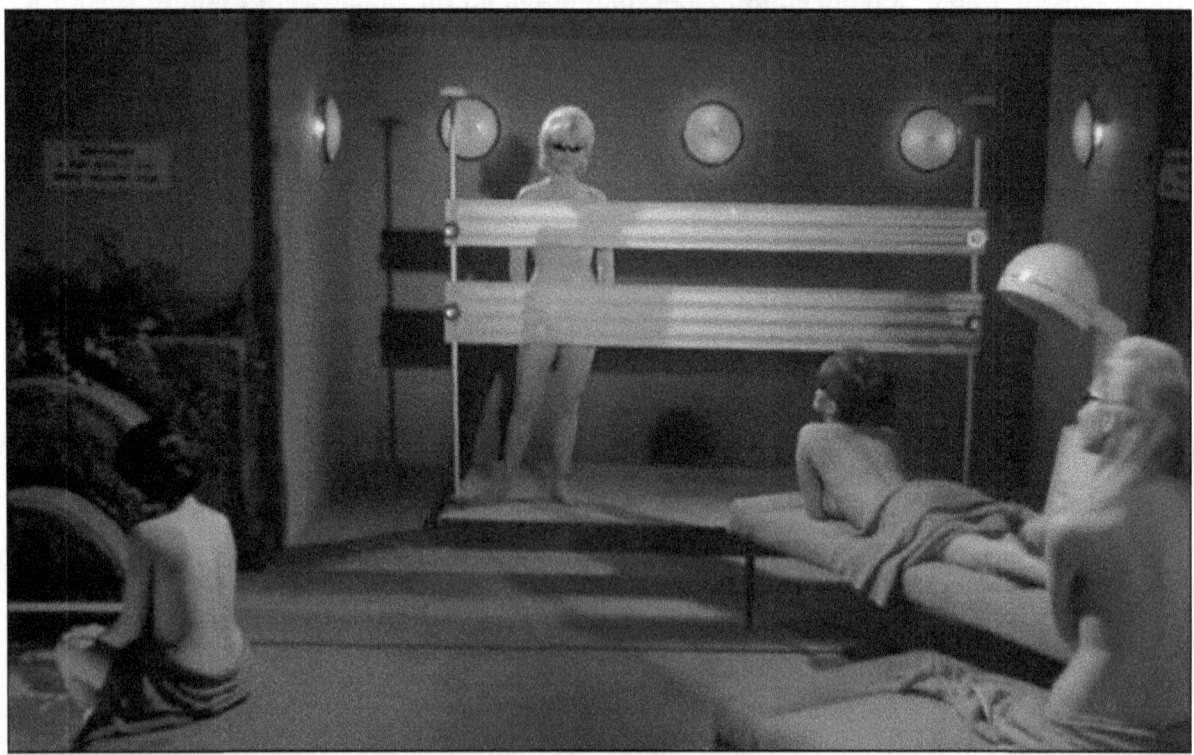

In the year 2071, Merry Anders as Carol White (behind screen) relaxes in the women's quarters while sharing some girl talk with Reena, played by Delores Wells (under towel). The future seemed to be a pretty thrilling place in 1964. Now we know better.

Forry Ackerman shows how to square a circle. A fun aspect of *Time Travelers* was the producers' insistence on showing what amounted to magic tricks done up as super science on screen and in real time.

Merry Anders...

...and Delores Wells provided the eye candy for *Time Travelers*.

After stepping through into the future, our cast looks back into the time screen at their twentieth century lab. That's Philip Carey as Dr. Steve Connors, Merry Anders, and Preston Foster as Dr. Erik von Steiner.

The Last Man on Earth (1964)

An end of the world story in which everyone has been turned into vampires and only Vincent Price remains as the last human being on Earth. Was it horror or science fiction? In one sense, it was horror, having launched an endless string of imitations featuring populations that have either been changed into vampires or zombies who then chase down the last surviving humans, usually to eat them. In another sense, it was SF, as author Richard Matheson maintains (who wrote the novel upon which this film is based as well as the screenplay). Matheson based his claim on the fact that he'd devised a completely scientific rationale for his story's vampirism. Whichever it was, this Italian/American film is a low budget classic from its compelling opening half hour to its inventive story structure. Very close to the original novel, it nevertheless swerves away in the end, diluting Matheson's philosophical ending, a change that not only prompted the author to remove his name from the writing credits but which has unfortunately served as the template from which at least two subsequent, and inferior, sequels were made.

The conclusion of *Last Man on Earth* veered from Matheson's original but still retained some of its religio-philosophical sub-text. Here, Vincent Price as Dr. Robert Morgan, is about to become extinct by a new species of human being.

Robert Morgan's home is besieged by vampires thirsting for his blood.

Vincent Price as Robert Morgan could have done worse than finding Franca Bettoia as the last woman on Earth! Alas! Her fair looks lasted only so long as she took a serum that kept the vampire infection at bay.

Uselessly, Robert Morgan goes through the motions of hunting down and killing vampires then burning their remains in a pit outside the city.

Arriving home late, Robert Morgan nearly succumbs to the vampires.

Children of the Damned (1964)

Solid but at times pedantic sequel to *Village of the Damned* based on *The Midwich Cuckoos*, a book by SF writer John Wyndham. Crisp b/w cinematography and on location scenes help build atmosphere but not much is done with the concept of children with vast mental powers given them through mysterious births (the male part of the equation is nowhere in sight). What gives? Film has quite disturbing opening sequence though and an ending that casts doubt on whether the government was responsible in ridding the world of the children's menace or the children themselves were.

They're baaaack! This time with an international cast.

Clive Powell as Paul, spokesman for the hybrid children.

British officials interview Paul and realize the danger the children pose to the world.

Powerful and disturbing opening scene to *Children of the Damned* when Paul attempts to kill his mother by forcing her to walk into traffic.

Tomb of Ligeia (1964)

Roger Corman's last and most ambitious in his series of Edgar Allen Poe adaptations is as lush and atmospheric as any of his previous efforts but moves at a snail's pace. Beautifully photographed on location at a burned out abbey in England, most of the action moves indoors where the usual cobweb bedecked set takes over. Hampered with by now familiar Corman tropes such as winding secret passages, the castle being destroyed in a climactic scene of fire and brimstone, and leading man Vincent Price once again obsessing over a dead relative this time his first wife who happened to be a witch. Second wife Elizabeth Shepherd is forceful and attractive but soon assumes helplessness as her husband's strange behavior intensifies (how she could have been attracted by Price's cadaverous appearance in the first place is anyone's guess!) Fun and atmospheric (or at least as much atmosphere as over lit sets can muster…the viewer is supposed to believe all that light comes from a few candles!) the film is worth viewing purely as a quality Corman offering…and Price's recitation of Poe's "Ligeia" is nice too.

The cadaverous Vincent Price as Verden Fell, still carrying a torch for his dead first wife.

Verden Fell's first wife , Ligeia, whose preserved face can still be seen through a window in her coffin!

Don't ask what lovely Elizabeth Shepherd as Rowena Fell saw in Verden Fell, we have no idea!

Under the spell of Ligeia, Verden Fell attempts to kill second wife Rowena.

Planet of the Vampires (1965)

Director of popular horror films such as *Black Sunday*, Italian director Mario Bava began his career as a set designer and FX man. Both skill sets would seem to have made him the perfect choice to direct this science fiction effort originally titled "Terror in Space." And Bava does do a good job establishing mood and atmosphere supported by eerie sets and production design (great costumes!) but some poor outer space FX prevent the film from being a complete success. Bava is partially to blame with some frankly uninspired and sometimes confusing direction. As usual for ambitious European productions, low budget American stars were imported to give the film a veneer of legitimacy including Barry Sullivan as Capt. Mark Markary. Unfortunately, Sullivan can't help a mostly wooden cast that viewers quickly lose track of as they're killed off one by one. But even with all that, the film is a great deal of fun and was a major influence on later American SF film makers especially one called *Alien*...

Classic scene from *Planet of Vampires* as dead crewmen rise from their graves. Color was an important factor in set design and production adding to the spookiness of this scene which director Bava filmed in slow motion.

A crewman is startled by a sound in the fog enshrouded landscape…

Evi Marandi as Tonia and Norma Bengell as Sanya round out the distaff members of the luckless astronauts in *Planet of the Vampires*.

Stylish costumes and sets are among the notable attractions of *Planet of the Vampires*.

Die, Monster, Die! (1965)

"It looks like a zoo in hell!" exclaims Nick Adams upon seeing a menagerie of monstrous mutations filling a shut up greenhouse operated by Boris Karloff. The scene perfectly captures the weird atmosphere of this Roger Corman-like gem, a very loose adaptation of H.P. Lovecraft's story "The Colour Out of Space." Despite the unnecessary relocation of the action from a remote New England farmhouse to the English countryside, the film nevertheless works on its own merits as old Nahum Witley (played by Karloff) tries to make up for his family's history of madness and debauchery. To do it, he conducts experiments with radioactive fragments from a fallen meteor but all that results are man eating giant plants (even though the only morsel they attempt to feed on is lovely Suzan Farmer playing Nahum's daughter Susan Witley) and mutated animals. As a side effect, radiation from the fragments is causing everyone in the house to die a horrible death of physical decomposition (much as they did in the original story). Enter young outsider Nick Adams as Stephen Reinhart who has come to take Susan away with him, thus involving himself in the mystery surrounding Witley and his experiments. The opening scenes of Reinhart's arrival in the town of Arkham, his walk across the countryside and over the "blasted heath" where the meteor has fallen, and the fog enshrouded woodland around the old house are all wonderfully evocative making up for the fiery ending which by this time had become de rigeur in contemporaneous Corman films. A fun movie directed by Daniel Haller and scripted by Jerry Sohl that, except for *The Dunwich Horror*, was for many years the best adaptation of H.P. Lovecraft to film.

Susan Farmer en dishabillier. No wonder Nick Adams risked it all to take her from the old Witley place!

Nick Adams was already a popular star by the time of *Die, Monster, Die* having starred in his own TV show, *The Rebel*.

"A zoo in hell!" Nick Adams as Stephen Reinhart and Suzan Farmer as Susan Witley make a disturbing discovery in the greenhouse: Cthulhoid monsters!

Cool matte shot of Nick Adams crossing the blasted heath in *Die, Monster, Die!* In the story, it was created after a meteor slammed onto the Witley estate.

Stephen Reinhart is threatened by an irradiated Nahum Witley.

Curse of the Fly (1965)

Superior effort to its immediate sequel, *Curse* opens strongly with a provocative scene involving a half naked woman making her escape from an asylum and being picked up by motorist Martin Delambre (George Baker), grandson of David Hedison's character in the original movie. In quick time, the two fall in love and are married, much to the annoyance of Baker's father, Henri Delambre (Brian Donlevy), who has good reason for being upset. You see, he and his sons are involved in experiments with matter transferral and have not stopped with inanimate objects. The results of their experiments, including Baker's first wife, are kept locked up in cells behind the big, spooky mansion. As sequels go, this one was pretty interesting, daring to deviate somewhat from its predecessors and taking the horror explored in the first film to the next level. Black and white direction by Don Sharp that avoids use of the back lot is moody and effective and music by Bert Shefter adds to the overall weird effect. Pretty good!

Carole Gray as Patricia Stanley makes her escape from the insane asylum at the start of *Curse of the Fly*.

Patricia Stanley explores the grounds of her new home. Behind the doors are held prisoner the experimental failures of the teleporter device including her predecessor in her husband's affections!

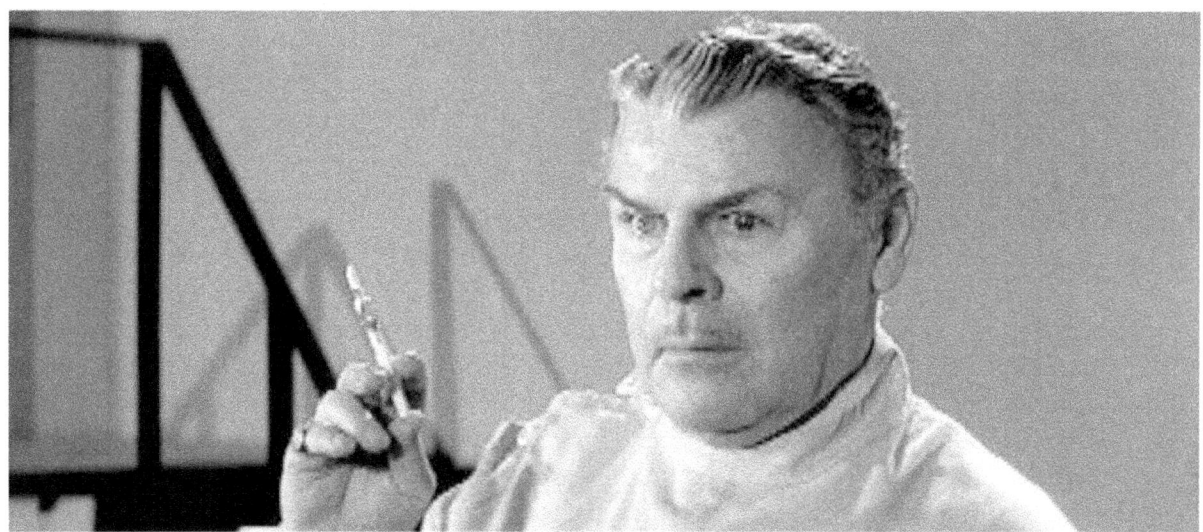

Brian Donlevy as Henri Delambre doing his best to appear as a mad scientist…and succeeding!

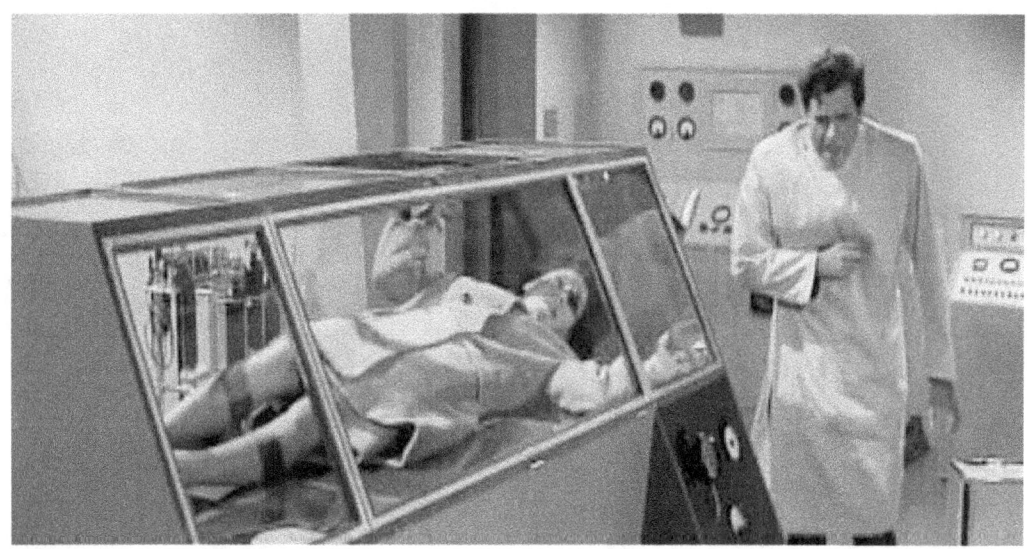

Another victim of science…sorry. Another giant step forward for science!

Mrs. Delambre, meet the first Mrs. Delambre…

Incubus (1966)

Moody, atmospheric but ultimately dull experimental film by *Outer Limits* co-creator Leslie Stevens. Although the film features a pre-*Star Trek* William Shatner, the real star of the movie is Dominic Frontiere whose inventive score (that nevertheless sounded in many places like leftover bits from the *Outer Limits*) goes a long way to making this story about a demoness who tries and fails to corrupt a good man a real atmospheric tour de force. Aiding Frontiere is Conrad Hall, also an *Outer Limits* alumnus, whose black and white cinematography is pure eye candy. Having all the dialogue spoken in the kooky invented language of Esperanto only adds to the overall weirdness but in the final measure, prevents the film from crossing the line into marketability. Written and wonderfully directed by Stevens (the opening sequence is particularly unsettling), the film is a noble attempt and a strange masterpiece that was lost for decades before being recently rediscovered.

The music of Dominic Frontiere went a long way to creating the weird atmosphere that predominates *Incubus*.

Conrad Hall went on to win multiple Academy Awards for cinematography But before all that, he made *The Outer Limits* and *Incubus* a joy to genre fans!

The disturbing opening sequence of *Incubus* that foreshadows the fate of William Shatner's Marc should he succumb to the wiles of demons.

Young demoness Allyson Ames as Kia (right) is given her mission by Eloise Hardt as Amael to corrupt the soul of Marc. Their plans go awry however when Kia falls in love with her victim.

Fantastic Voyage (1966)

From the mid 1960s through the mid 70s, Hollywood managed to produce a second wave of SF films that not only introduced viewers to all kinds of science fiction concepts but presented them in a newly mature manner. These films were aimed not primarily at kids, but adult audiences. *Fantastic Voyage* was the first in this new line of modern films that nevertheless were immensely entertaining. And with a plot involving shrinking a team of physicians and their accompanying submarine to the size of a microbe so that they can operate on a dying man from the inside of his brain, how could it be anything else? Structured around a single solid SF concept supported by FX that manage to capture a true sense of wonder, this film, directed by Richard Fleischer, can't help but keep viewers enthralled. All of it is topped off with a healthy admiration of God when chief scientist Arthur Kennedy sees no other explanation for the perfection of human biology but that there must be a "creative intelligence at work." In between, the team led by stalwart Stephen Boyd must battle ravenous white corpuscles and treacherous saboteurs in order to complete its life or death mission. They don't make 'em like this anymore!

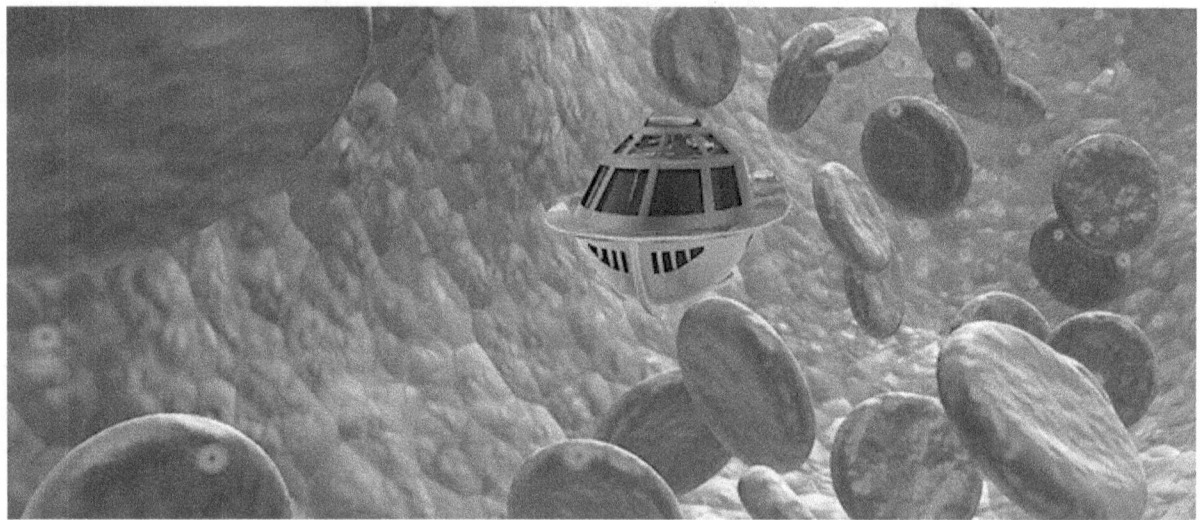

The miniaturized *Proteus* travels through the blood stream on its way to the brain. No way can simple black and white convey the dazzling FX as the original color film can!

The crew of the *Proteus* looks on dazzled as they travel through the blood stream. Can there be any doubt that there is "creative intelligence" at work?

Our all star cast prepares to embark on a "Fantastic Voyage:" Raquel Welch as lab assistant Cora Peterson, Arthur Kennedy as brain surgeon Dr. Peter Duval, Donald Pleasance as Dr. Michaels, Stephen Boyd as government agent Charles Grant.

The surgical team prepares to operate from inside the brain using a laser gun as a scalpel! For sheer imaginative excellence, it'd be hard to beat *Fantastic Voyage*!

Edmund O'Brien as Gen. Carter and Arthur O'Connell as Col. Reid track the *Proteus* from outside the patient's body.

One Million Years B.C. (1966)

Okay, not every SF movie from the mid 1960s on was top flight. And if it wasn't for some sparse stop motion effects by Ray Harryhausen and its iconic shots of top billed star Raquel Welch in a fur bikini, this film would be largely a waste of time for any viewer. Whatever entertainment value the movie has derives mainly from its wealth of scientific errors and historical inaccuracies. An attempt to stitch it all together with some stone age soap opera only adds to the general hilarity. For Harryhausen fans only.

One good reason to like *One Million Years B.C.* Raquel Welch as cave girl Loana!

...and another good reason... Lisa Thomas as cave girl Sura.

Primitive lovers: Ralph Richardson as the crude Tumak and Raquel Welch as more refined Loana.

Ralph Richardson as Tumak faces down a baby Tyranosaurus.

Due to time constraints and budget, FX director Ray Harryhausen was not above using old fashioned methods such as this composition shot with an actual lizard standing in for a dinosaur.

Children and cave girls first! A giant turtle menaces our cast!

Fahrenheit 451 (1966)

Good example of why SF moviemaking should be left to the experts, namely American studios! Noted French director Francois Truffaut plus an adaptation of science fiction author Ray Bradbury's most famous novel should have added up to greatness but instead misses by a country mile. Truffaut, who also had a hand in the script, manages to take Bradbury's scary dystopian future where freedom of thought is suppressed and books burned and turn it into a dull mess without dollar one to spend. Stars Oskar Werner (who he?) as conscience ridden fireman Guy Montag and Julie Christie in the dual role of Montag's wife and underground siren Clarisse McClellan do little to inject feeling into the dreary goings on. Everyone's heart is in the right place, but that's cold comfort for audiences expecting more from this team. It does have somewhat of a moving ending though as we leave Montag among a colony of subversives busily memorizing books so they won't be lost forever. For completists only.

Ray Bradbury wrote *Fahrenheit 451* as a cautionary tale about the suppression of freedom of thought. More than ever, as massive corporations such as Google shut down dissent to the prevailing PC culture, the world is waiting for the definitive adaptation of his classic novel.

Director Francois Truffaut

A woman caught with a stash of forbidden books is set aflame by firemen in *Fahrenheit 451*.

At the climax of *Fahrenheit 451*, Oskar Werner (reading book) as Guy Montag and Julie Christie (in scarf) Clarisse McClellan walk among the book people memorizing their assigned books.

Seconds (1966)

Director John Frankenheimer manages to capture the surrealistic life of an older man who, dissatisfied with his empty existence, fakes his death and takes on a new identity. But the direction threatens to overwhelm an otherwise intriguingly told story with its odd camera angles and movements; strange, even somnabulent pacing; and deceptively sinister performances by Jeff Corey and Will Geer as the operators behind a group that offers new lives for the bored well to do…for a price. And sometimes, when a customer fails to adapt to his new life, that price can be the ultimate one which supplies this film its horrific ending. The horror is further underlined with the casting of H-wood heart throb Rock Hudson as the new persona assumed by a disaffected John Randolph. After being seduced by the bohemian lifestyle created for him by the group, Hudson's character breaks down and insists on starting over with a new identity. That's when the fine print of his agreement with the group finally does him in. A strange, paranoid film that is also a cautionary tale on the empty promises of modern materialism. (Adult content)

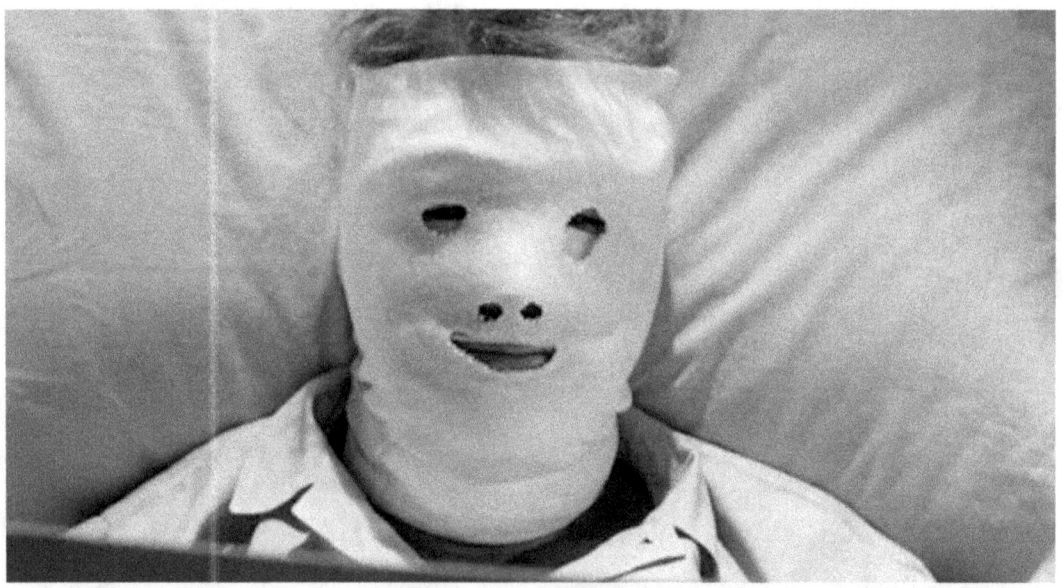

Rock Hudson as he awakens from the operation that will give him a new, youthful look and ultimately a new identity.

Creepy Jeff Corey eats lunch while telling John Randolph about his coming transformation.

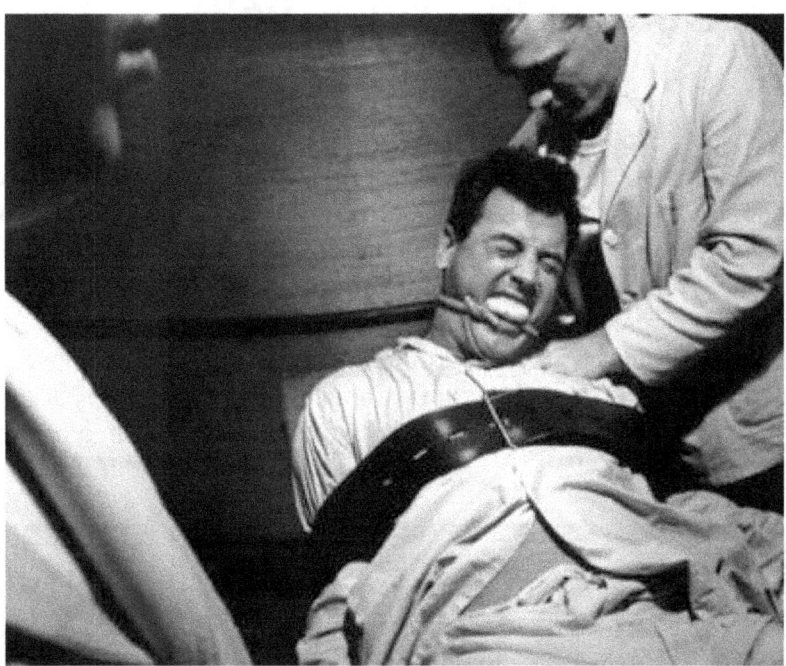

Shocking climax to *Seconds* as Rock Hudson's Tony Wilson finally realizes what the small print in his contract means…

The honey trap: Salome Jens as Nora Marcus played Tony Wilson's romantic interest in *Seconds* and his lead in to the bohemian lifestyle planned for him.

2001: A Space Odyssey (1968)

Shattering viewers' expectations in traditional SF fare, this film still manages to harken back to earlier efforts at realism such as *Conquest of Space* and *Project Moonbase*. At the same time, its cerebral approach to the subject of space travel became the antithesis of later science fantasies popularized by *Star Wars*. While its script is built around a single concept, it's nevertheless a big one! Nothing less than man carried to the next stage of evolution, a stage destined to be as far removed from what man is now as he is to his ape forbears. Really, in almost every respect, ideas, FX, story, direction, and influence on subsequent SF cinema (will we ever listen to the *Blue Danube* again without a slowly rotating space station coming immediately to mind?) this movie has it all, but what holds this one back from the number one spot is that even to its fans, it's just not that much fun! Good brain food though!

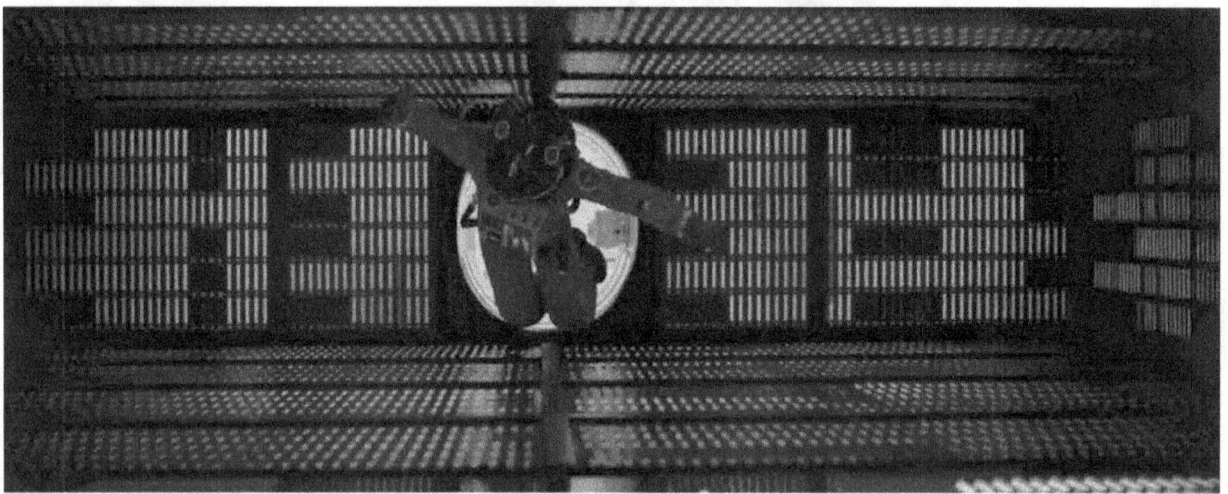

Keir Dullea as astronaut David Bowman, enters the HAL computer to shut it down. In the movie, the computer breaks down and kills the entire crew of the Jupiter mission and at least tries to do the same to Bowman.

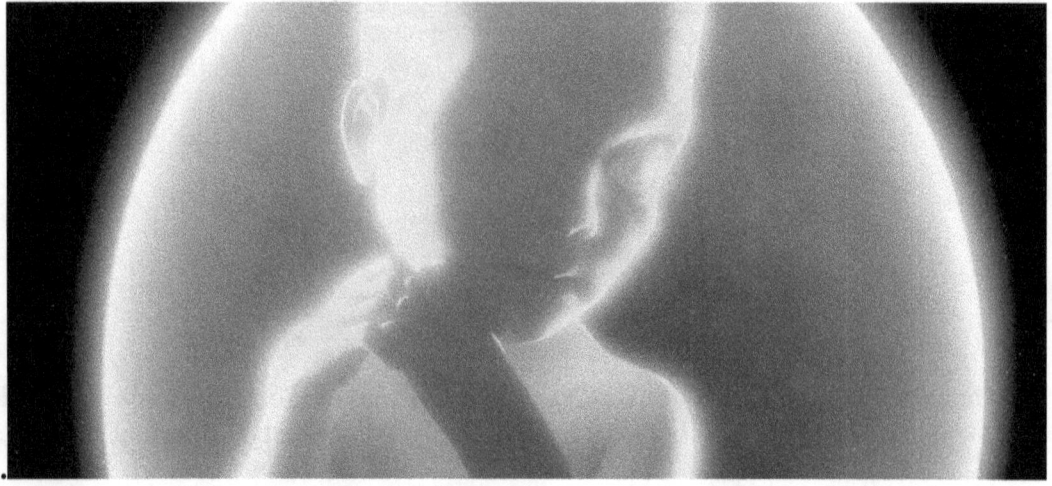

The "star child" representative of the next step in the evolution of man as it appears at the conclusion of *2001*.

Tricks of the trade: the interior set of the *Discovery One*...

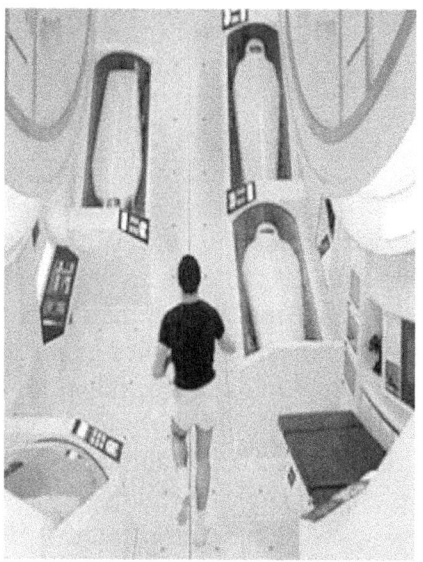

....and as it appears in the film with Bowman seen jogging around its interior under seemingly near zero gravity.

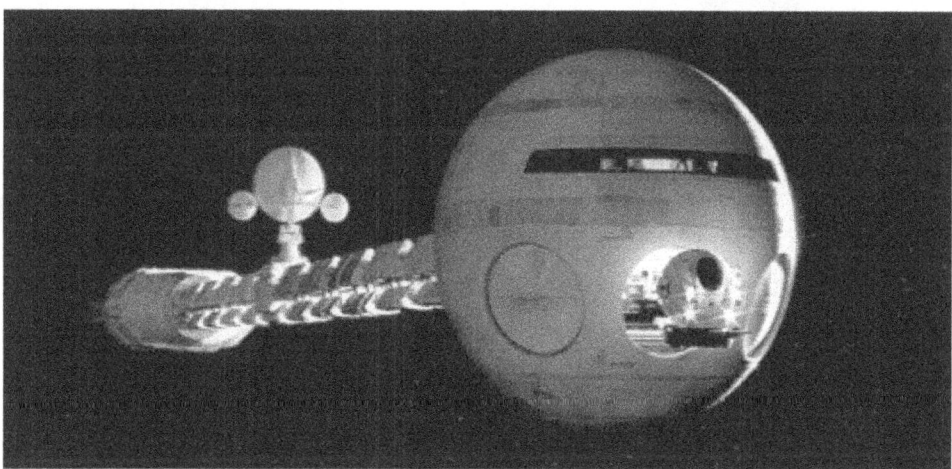

Exterior of the *Discovery One* with EVA pod being launched

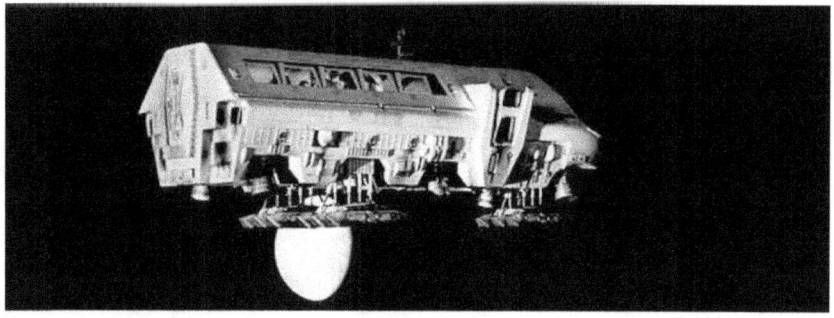

The Moon Bus is an example of how *2001*'s model designs changed the look of spaceships in SF movies forever after.

The Planet of the Apes (1968)

One of the purest of all sixties SF films filled with unforgettable scenes from the opening hunt to the final, iconic shot of the Statue of Liberty. Intensely cynical in outlook, the film is nevertheless filled with neat ideas not least of which is a topsy-turvy world where apes are the dominant species and man is relegated near the bottom! Charlton Heston makes a smooth transition from the epics he made in the fifties to the SF genre and is frequently maligned for his acting in this film which, for the life of us, we can't see! It's ironic that Heston's character, the misanthropic Taylor, is forced to defend humanity throughout the film only to discover that his initial cynicism about it was well placed! Adapted by Rod Serling from the novel by Pierre Boule, the apish elements of the film are complemented by a truly inventive score from Jerry Goldsmith. A series of sequels begun in (2011) has managed to live up to the promise of the original...so far!

"Damn them all to hell!" The iconic final scene in *Planet of the Apes*

Linda Harrison as Nova provided the eye candy for *Planet of the Apes* as well as someone for Taylor to talk to.

One of the few instances in film history where nudity was justified. Charlton Heston as Taylor goes on trial. If an ape were placed on trial in our world, would it be required to wear clothes?

Role reversal was a big part of *Planet of the Apes*. Here, ape hunters, beat through a corn field to flush out wild humans.

The Power (1968)

Brought to you by producer George Pal and director Byron Haskin, the same team that gave you *The War of the Worlds*, the film presents a faithful adaptation of the classic novel by Frank M. Robinson. Underscored with a haunting theme by Miklos Rosa, the story tells of a powerful mutant whose ESP powers give him virtually the power of a god as he kills off anyone who might suspect his existence. Is he the first of a new race of men destined to replace mere homo sapiens or simply an anomaly corrupted by his vast abilities? You be the judge as you follow George Hamilton and Suzanne Pleshette (not to mention such genre faves as Richard Carlson, Earl Holliman, Michael Rennie, and Gary Merrill) as they frantically search like mice in a maze for the truth and the identity of the man with...the power!

George Hamilton as Prof. James Tanner is given a preview of any number of ways that superhuman Michael Rennie as Adam Hart could decide to kill him.

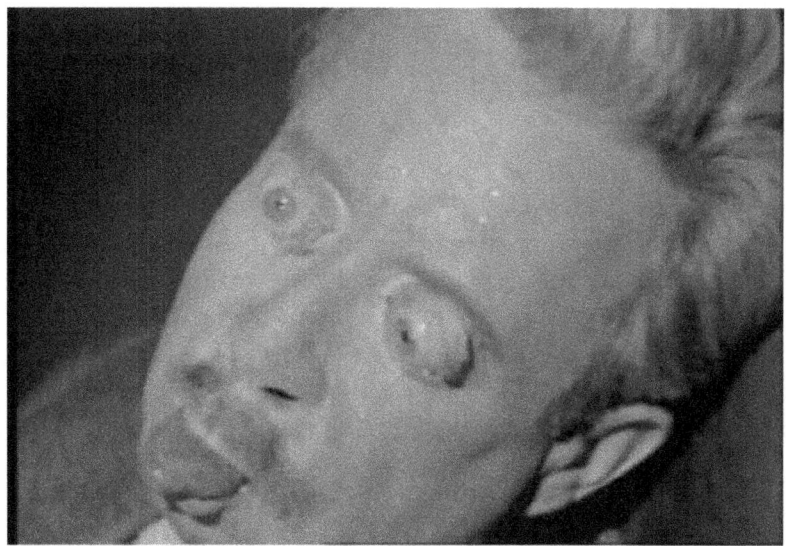

Gruesome image of Arthur O'Connell as Prof. Henry Hallson. It was Hallson's questionnaire of his fellow researchers that revealed the existence of the super human in their midst. Inadvertently, the questionnaire revealed to Adam Hart that there was a second super human in existence, prompting him to begin eliminating the group of researchers one by one beginning with the unfortunate Hallson who was first asphyxiated, then squashed in an out of control centrifuge!

George Hamilton as Prof. James Tanner confronts Aldo Ray as Bruce, a mechanic left behind in Adam Hart's birthplace to kill anyone who came asking about him. Bruce had left Tanner for dead in the middle of an Air Force bombing range, so Tanner's angry looks here are perhaps justified! Throughout, *The Power* provides a strong SF concept around which suspense builds to the surprising climax. For its ideas and execution, one of the best sci fi films ever made.

Five Million Miles to Earth (1968)

Known in the UK as *Quatermass and the Pit*, this film features a clever idea for an SF yarn. To wit: humanity has been genetically engineered from a dying race of Martian grasshoppers with all our violent, even racist, tendencies having been programmed into us! Peppered with lots of small revelations, the story moves along at a good clip but is somewhat vitiated by a big monster finish (later ripped off in the cheesy *Lifeforce*). Although Andrew Keir as Quatermass was a step down from Brian Donlevy, beautiful Barbara Shelley more than makes up for the substitution! Overall, still a solid entry in the Quatermass films.

After a subway construction crew find what they think is an unexploded bomb from WWII, the army ordinance is called in. They soon discover that what they have is not a bomb but an alien spacecraft...one that's still occupied!

Andrew Keir as Prof. Quatermass and James Donald as Dr. Matthew Roney remove one of the alien bodies from the alien ship.

Lovely Barbara Shelley as Barbara Judd went a long way in making up for the fact of not having Brian Donlevy around as Quatermass.

Andrew Keir's wide eyed Quatermass lacked the single minded detachment that made Brian Donlevy's portrayal unique in the annals of SF cinema.

Valley of the Gwangi (1969)

Although somewhat slow to start, this entry does feature an intriguing mix of cowboys and dinosaurs sure to catch anyone's attention. In it, ne'er do well James Franciscus travels south of the border hoping to revive a relationship with ex-girlfriend and wild west show owner Gila Golan. Instead, he finds ringmaster Richard Carlson, a gypsy dwarf, and a hidden valley filled with rampaging dinosaurs! Although lighting problems make for jarring contrasts in many of the early stop motion scenes (one of which includes a spectacular sequence of cowboys roping a Tyrannosaurus Rex), Ray Harryhausen's stop motion effects eventually triumph in the scene where the T-Rex finds itself trapped in a cathedral! Fun facts: this was Harryhausen's last use of dinosaurs in stop motion. After *Gwanji,* the animator would focus his energies exclusively on purely fantasy based FX. Harryhausen worked on *Gwanji* as sort of a tribute to mentor Willis O'Brien who had intended to produce the project for himself.

Close up of *Gwanji*'s spectacular FX scene where cowboys rope a T-rex!

Another flawless composite of cowboys in the same shot as the T-rex.

Gwangi goes to church: the fish out of water scenes of the T-rex stalking human prey in the cavernous confines of a cathedral were impressive.

Gila Golan as circus owner TJ Breckinridge, wasn't just set decoration on *Gwanji*, she also provided it with a feisty but still feminine lead that should've been the model for later genre heroines but wasn't.

James Franciscus played Tuck Kirby in *Gwanji*. He'd likely have become a genre regular if television hadn't called!

When Dinosaurs Ruled the Earth (1970)

When the big returns came in for *One Million Years B.C.* it didn't take a rock to fall on the heads of producers at Hammer Films! Almost immediately, they launched a second cave girl extravaganza with *When Dinosaurs Ruled the Earth*. Like its predecessor, the film featured plenty of fur bikini clad lovelies, chief among them Victoria Vetri as Sanna who does Raquel Welch one better by completely disrobing for some quick skinny dipping with Cro Magnon hunk Robin Hawdon as Tara. The plot involves the usual prehistoric silliness of human sacrifice, beauty taming a beast, and the invention of romantic love (hard to believe this film was directed by Val Guest and scripted by SF author J.G. Ballard…but it was!) The real attraction to this otherwise skippable film however, is the stop animation FX by one Jim Danforth who has the distinction of being practically the only other name to be mentioned in company with forbears Willis O'Brien and Ray Harryhausen. And judging from his sophisticated work here, Danforth is indeed worthy of being in such company. Bottom line: see it for the stop motion dinosaurs! (Adult content)

Beautiful FX shot as Sanna befriends…well, some kind of dinosaur!

A stop motion sequence with an attacking land crab was actually disturbing.

Me Sanna, you Tara! Victoria Vetri in the mandatory fur bikini and co-star Robin Hawdon get to know each other.

Human sacrifice was one of life's hazards *When Dinosaurs Ruled the Earth*!

Animator Jim Danforth.

The Dunwich Horror (1970)

An adaptation of the H.P. Lovecraft story of the same name isn't bad with some moments of genuine invention and weirdness. In fact, it's likely the best treatment of Lovecraft on the big screen before the rise of the independent film scene of the 21st century. The inclusion of Sandra Dee and the plot to have her impregnated with the child of Yog Sothoth is however, unfortunate. (Adult content)

If *The Dunwich Horror* was at all effective as weird cinema, one of the reasons has to be Dean Stockwell as Wilbur Whately. His depiction of the young devil worshipper was both intense and crazed with little unexpected touches of strangeness added in.

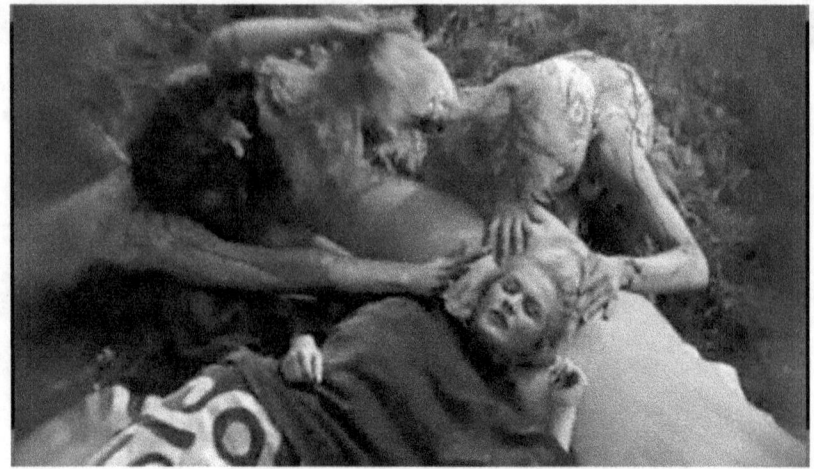

Psychedelic dream sequences had become de riguer for sixties cinema. In this one, Sandra Dee as the hapless Nancy Wagner is harassed by crazed cultists!

Nice matte shot of the "devil's hopyard" in *The Dunwich Horror*.

Inventive shot of Donna Baccala as student Elizabeth Hamilton searching Wilbur's home. Her escapade will not end well.

Sandra Dee was on the reverse slope of her career when she performed as Nancy Wagner in *The Dunwhich Horror*.

Colossus: The Forbin Project (1970)

So good it had to have two titles! Perfect SF film and adaptation from the novel by D. F. Jones about a super computer buried beneath the Rocky Mountains that takes over the world by holding it hostage to the nuclear missiles foolishly entrusted to it by its creator, Dr. Charles Forbin played by Eric Braeden. Expertly paced by director Joseph Sargent, the film hasn't a single dull moment one of which features the cleverest reasons any film ever used to justify a bed scene: under constant surveillance by Colossus, Forbin convinces the machine of his need for regular visits by his "mistress" (played by lovely Susan Clark) who is actually his co-worker. In the privacy of Forbin's bedroom, with all of Colossus' video and audio units turned off, pillow talk consists of the two exchanging information on efforts to defeat the computer! Another impressive scene occurs earlier in the film when Colossus attempts to contact its Russian opposite number and begins establishing a common means of communication. Here, reams of mathematical information cascades across a pair of computer screens as Michael Colombier's unique score underlines the wonder of the moment. Featuring one of the best SF concepts ever to be translated to the screen, the film climaxes with the chilling voice of Colossus informing the world that it has a new master: "We can co-exist but only on my terms. You will say you lose your freedom but freedom is an illusion. In time, you will come to regard me not only with respect and awe, but with love." (Adult content)

Eric Braeden as Dr. Forbin walks the last mile inside the guts of Colossus before turning on the computer and locking himself and anyone else out of it for all time…big mistake!

Colossus establishes a basis for communication with its counterpart in the Soviet Union.

Attractive Susan Clark as Dr. Cleo Markham made film history in a bed scene from *Colossus: The Forbin Project*. It not only made sense for the plot, but was done in a sensible, tasteful manner.

Colossus clear: the President, played by Gordon Pinsent in Kennedy like style, gets the bad news that he isn't in charge anymore.

No one defies Colossus! Two Forbin Project scientists are ordered executed by the super computer for plotting against it.

Beneath the Planet of the Apes (1970)

Definitely a big step down from the first film in the series (but a step up from the remaining three), this sequel still manages to deliver some good Saturday matinee style entertainment. James Franciscus is properly intense and incredulous as the hero and Charlton Heston returns to blow up the world in the final scene. Filled with coincidences, paradoxes, plot holes, and lapses in logic, none of it makes much difference as the story of a followup space flight delivers Franciscus to the exact same ape village where Heston had been held captive and he proceeds to go through much the same paces. Eventually, he's chased into the Forbidden Zone where he finds traces of a ruined New York City, a hidden band of bomb worshipping mutants ("Glory be to the bomb and the holy fallout!"), and a captive Heston. Great hokum!

Linda Harrison reprises her role of Nova from the first film while James Franciscus as Brent fills in for Charlton Heston in *Beneath the Planet of the Apes*…at least until the real Heston shows up near the end.

All together now…everybody sing! "Praise be to the holy fallout!" Mutants worship a nuclear bomb.

Beneath did have its share of fun FX. Take this shot of Brent and Nova walking through the ruins of New York City for instance.

Brent and Taylor are forced to fight through mutant mind power. The effort fails and they make their escape.

Apes prepare to attack the mutant lair! Here, James Gregory as Gen. Ursus prepares to lead his army to victory.

THX 1138 (1971)

Before there was *Star Wars*, there was *THX 1138*, director George Lucas' first, and much more serious attempt at science fiction. Despite some logical inconsistencies, this film of a dystopian future society where everyone is controlled by an oppressive state through the use of mind and emotion deadening drugs while at the same time are inexplicably encouraged to shop till they drop, the slow to develop story is somehow compelling. Robert Duvall is THX who rebels against his programming when his roommate LUH 3417 is taken away from him and eventually escapes out of the city. Along the way, Lucas manages to address any number of SF concepts from the role of religion to society, sex, government, the drug culture, and the institutionalization of consumerism. Not that they're handled that well…as previously stated, the film is often confused and contradictory…but it remains a strong addition to an apocalyptic genre explored in other SF films such as *Soylent Green, Planet of the Apes,* and *Logan's Run.* The low budget film was enhanced to good effect decades later with a CGI gloss that has succeeded in making it much more watchable. (Adult content)

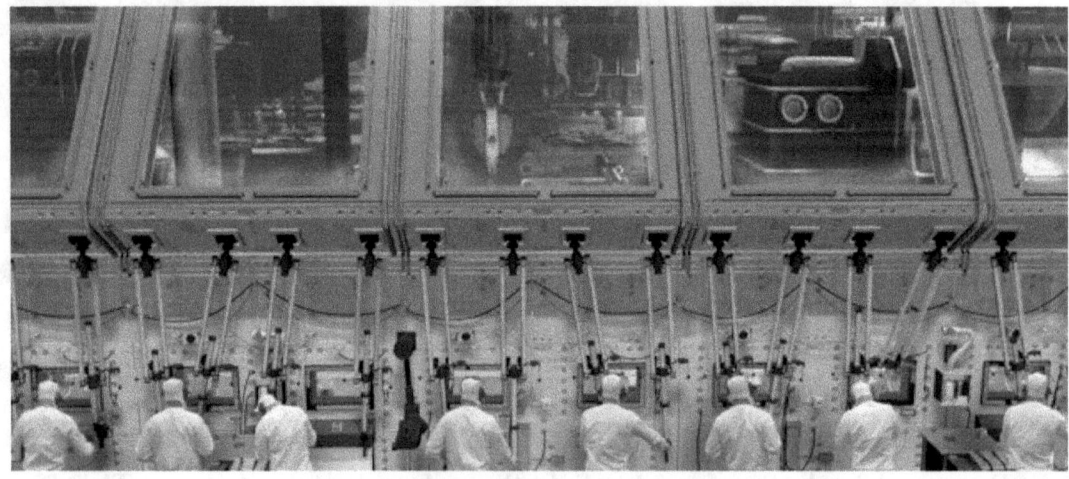

In an image reminiscent of Fritz Lang's *Metropolis,* workers in *THX 1138* labor in a lab using radioactive machine parts. This was one of the scenes later enhanced with CGI.

THX played by Robert Duvall and LUR played by Maggie McOmie find forbidden love in a dystopian future where emotions are vigorously suppressed.

Anyone looking for the kind of big gun action in *THX 1138* that would become routine in later years will come away disappointed. This brief car chase at the end of the movie when THX escapes from the city is about all that can be expected.

Donald Pleasance as SEN 5241 stumbles past a poster of a generic Jesus used by the faceless administration to promote a bland state religion as a palliative for restlessness in the population.

The Andromeda Strain (1971)

The question: what if a space satellite returned to earth carrying an unknown, deadly plague? The answer: confine it within an elaborate underground facility beneath the Nevada desert along with a team of doctors and biologists until an antidote can be found! Faithfully adapted by Nelson Gidding from the novel by Michael Crichton (except for the inexplicable substitution of a woman for one of the male scientists) and directed by Robert Wise who, after decades in the business, was still nimble enough to employ such filmic techniques as intercutting, transposition, flashbacks and even flashforwards to tell the story. The result is a great medical thriller filled with wonderful moments including the opening sequence wherein two of the scientists retrieve the fallen satellite from a small town where, because it was tampered with by the local physician, the plague has been released killing everyone except a sterno drinking old man and a screaming newborn. The connection between the two will be the key to solving this scientific whodunit!

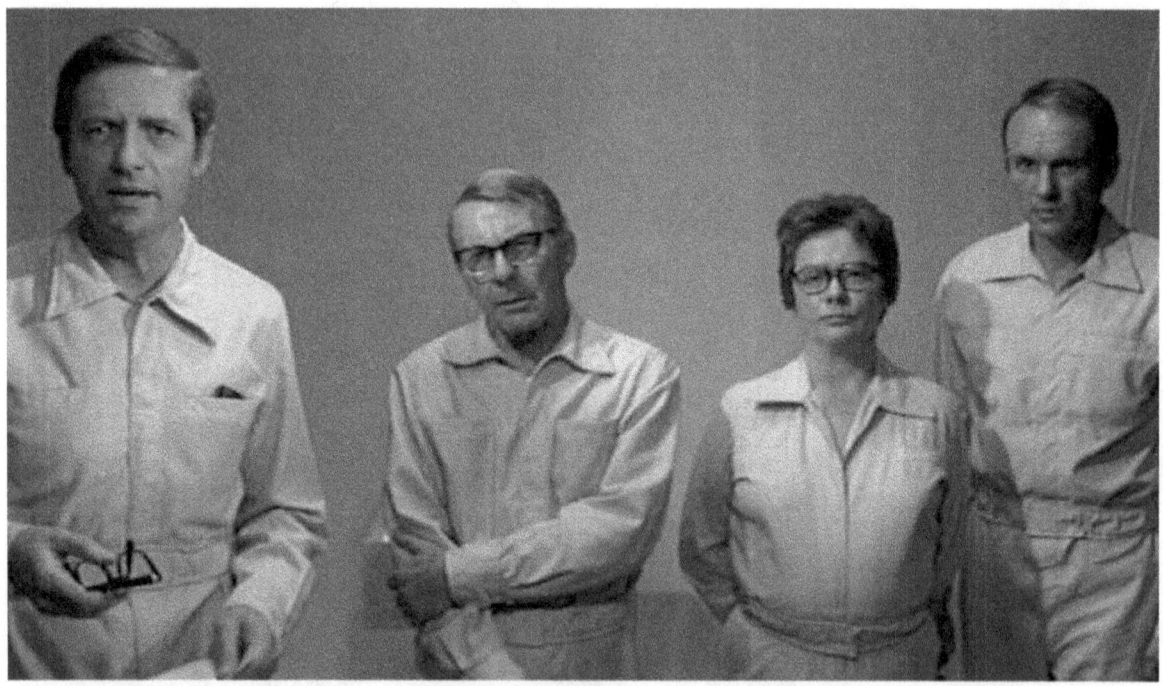

Our team of dauntless physicians and scientists charged with saving the world in *The Andromeda Strain*: **Arthur Hill as Dr. Jeremy Stone, David Wayne as Dr. Charles Dutton, Kate Reid as Dr. Ruth Leavitt, and James Olson as Dr. Mark Hall.**

Drs. Stone and Hall investigate the town where the *Andromeda Strain* was accidentally released after the local doctor opened a downed satellite.

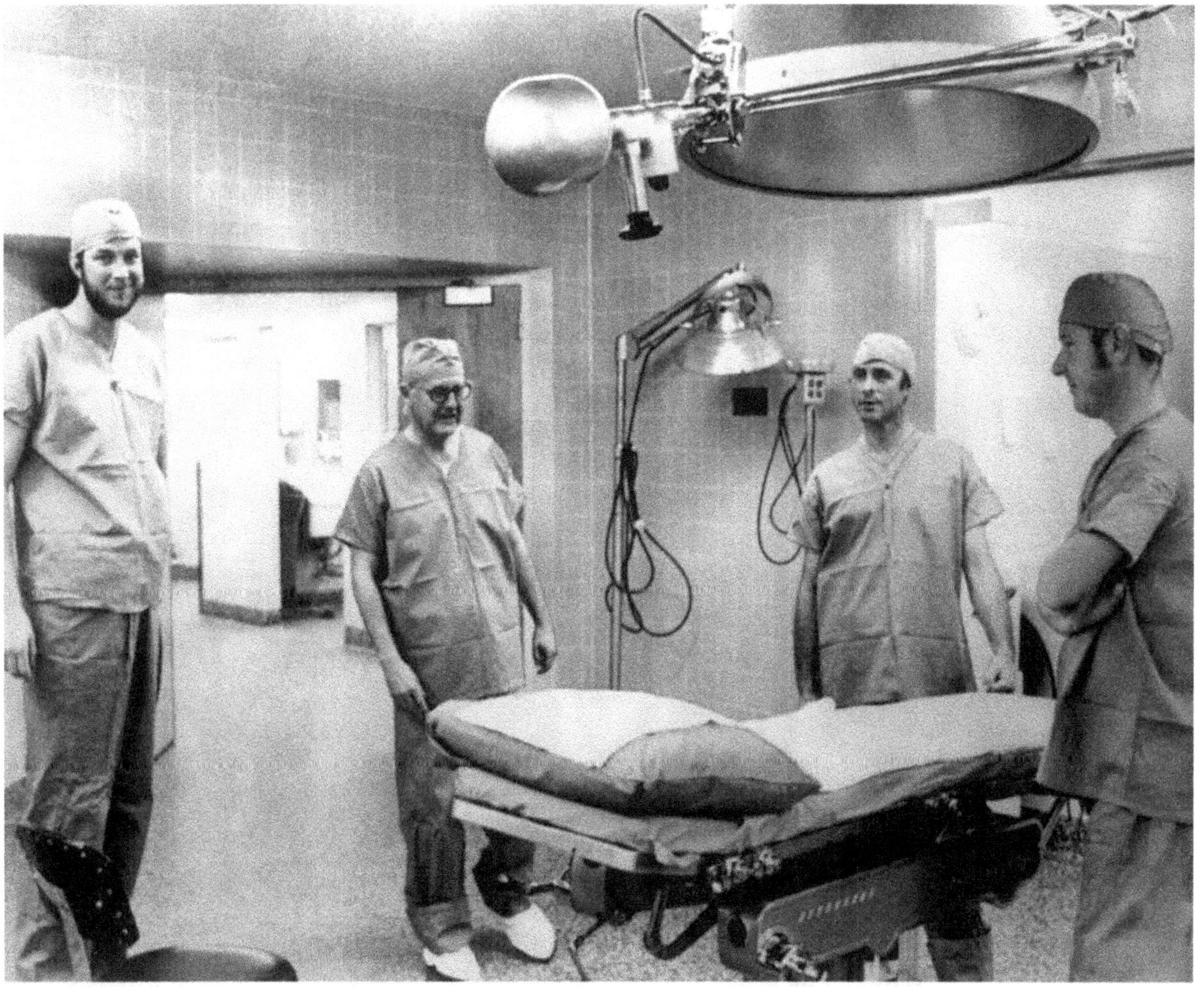

That's director Robert Wise second from left surveying an operating room set for the *Andromeda Strain* with author and later a director himself, Michael Crichton, on the left dressed for his non-speaking guest shot in the scene!

Duel (1971)

A young Steven Spielberg turns in a fine directorial effort over a Richard Matheson script (adapted from his story of the same name) that follows a typical California commuter as he becomes involved in every driver's nightmare: the prey of a mad 18-wheeled truck driver! Spielberg's first full length feature is, ironically, likely his best, *Duel* is a masterpiece of mounting suspense as hapless salesman David Mann (played by Dennis Weaver) is confronted with a series of increasingly dangerous situations as the faceless driver at the wheel of the monster truck tries his best to kill him. While not exactly SF or even fantasy, *Duel* still fills the bill with its mounting suspense and never seen truck driver making the murderous oil tanker seem more a force of nature or something supernatural than down to earth. The death groan of the crashing truck at the end is a marvelous touch suggesting as it does that the tanker may have been a living thing after all! Not strictly a theatrical film, it was later released in Europe as such as were other American made television films. But these movies were of such quality that they often outstripped their more expensive counterparts. And *Duel* is definitely one of those. A must see!

His big mistake: Dennis Weaver as David Mann honks impatiently at a slow moving truck. The most extreme instances of road rage quickly follows!

Dennis Weaver as David Mann tries to report the murderous truck driver to the police. Little does he know that his phone call is about to be cut short…!

David Mann looks fearfully over his shoulder as he realizes that the truck driver is intent on killing him and that he's on his own. Spielberg managed successfully to take the desert locations that Jack Arnold used for his SF films of the 1950s and updated their usage for audiences of the 1970s.

The Omega Man (1971)

Adapting to film Richard Matheson's classic novel *I Am Legend* was no doubt a good idea but something must have gone horribly wrong mid-way through the scripting process! What begins well with Charlton Heston hunting mutants by day and holding up in a brownstone turned fortress by night comes to a screeching halt roughly where the book ends…with Heston captured and prepared for execution by mutants who need to kill him before they can inherit the Earth. At that point, Heston is rescued by a jive talkin' Angela Davis lookalike and the film rapidly descends into an embarrassing, dated mess. *Omega Man*, however, does have some distinction, if you can call it that, of being the forerunner of every zombie movie made since. Moreso, than the previous version, *The Last Man on Earth* (which was a more satisfying version of the novel), because its use of mutants was much closer to the modern conception of the zombie than the scientific vampires of *Last Man*. (Adult content)

Spoiler alert: Iconic final shot of *Omega Man* with Charlton Heston in crucifixion pose. In a last minute directorial inclusion, Heston's Col. Robert Neville was depicted as mankind's savior due to it being his blood that will preserve humanity against the rise of the mutants. An ending diametrically opposite to that of Matheson's novel.

"Show him the marks!" Mutants display their disfigurements to Neville.

In the best scenes of the film, Charlton Heston as Neville, hunts down mutants during daylight hours.

In some of the most dated scenes in the film Rosalind Cash as Lisa leads a group of hippies in a commune-like lifestyle before revealing themselves to Neville.

Robert Neville picks off pesky mutants below his fortress like town house.

The Night Stalker (1972)

Not for nothing has this film been rated the highest ever for a made for TV movie! With a fast moving script by Richard Matheson set in present day Las Vegas and starring a virtual who's who of Hollywood stars (including Elisha Cook, Kent Smith, Ralph Meeker, Claud Akins, and Charles McGraw), this film was a revelation in the early seventies when it was first aired. Long before the 1990s vampire craze, its plot turning on what a vampire would be like if it "lived" in the modern United States is still compelling decades later. Made with a touch of black humor, star Darren McGavin as Carl Kolchak is perfect as the down on his luck reporter who doggedly follows up the clues and like Sherlock Holmes, concludes that when all other possibilities are eliminated, whatever is left, no matter how improbable must be the truth…in this case a 70 year old vampire! Although the impact of the film is somewhat muted due to 1970s TV production values, this film justly deserves its fearsome reputation and is a whole lot of fun besides!

Barry Atwater as Janos Skorzny, the modern day vampire, helps himself to some easy pickings…at the local blood bank!

Darren McGavin as Carl Kolchak played the role partially with tongue in cheek giving *The Night Stalker* the delicate balance it needed between seriousness and the absurd.

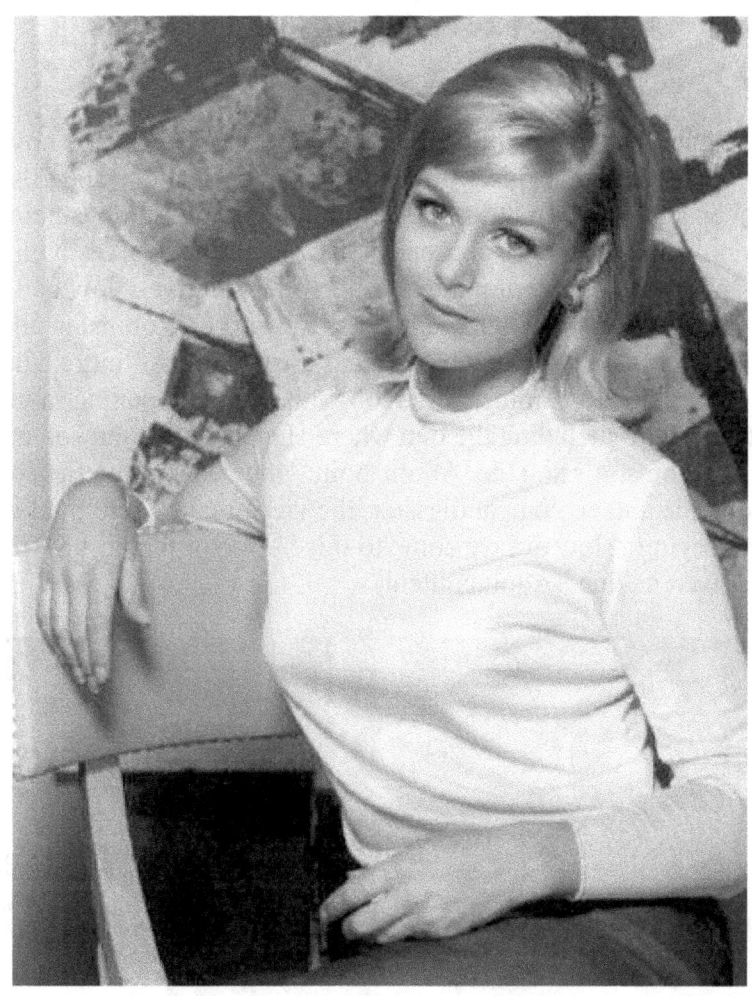

Adorable Carol Lynley as Gail Foster, Kolchak's girlfriend, gave *The Night Stalker* a boost when a breather was needed between scenes of blood curdling action or institutional intransigence!

Vampires weren't the only menaces Kolchak had to deal with in *The Night Stalker*: there was also a hostile officialdom and Tony Vincenzo, his long suffering editor played here by Simon Oakland.

Soylent Green (1973)

Unfairly maligned as an unfaithful adaptation of Harry Harrison's novel, the movie version is actually an improvement. Typical of the SF cinema of the 60s and 70s, it comes loaded with enough concepts for a dozen movies: overpopulation, pollution, suicide parlors, women as property, cannibalism, extreme conservation of natural resources, you name it. Expert set decoration and judicious use of mattes make up for relatively low budget and a solid cast headed by Charlton Heston, Chuck Connors, Edward G. Robinson, and Joseph Cotton helps move the murder mystery along while giving this dystopian future a human face. Director Richard Fleischer does a commendable job with a clever opening montage and a couple scenes that are truly moving including the one where Heston and Robinson enjoy a rare meal and later participate in Robinson's suicide. At one point, after witnessing the consequences of the world's economic and ecological disaster, the viewer can't help but be moved when Robinson breaks down saying "How did we come to this?" One of the best SF films of all time that has rarely been given its due. (Adult content)

"Soylent Green is people!" Charlton Heston as Det. Frank Thorn, makes the discovery while exploring a heavily guarded waste disposal facility.

***Soylent Green* is full of concepts including this scene giving an idea of how crowded the city has become: To leave his tiny apartment, Thorn must navigate people who pay to sleep in the corridors and stairwells!**

Crowd control in *Soylent Green*: mobs are broken up with trucks that scoop people up like so much garbage.

Leigh Taylor-Young starred as Shirl in *Soylent Green* but she was just "furniture" to the tenants she belonged to in the exclusive apartment complex where Heston's Det. Thorn was investigating the murder of a highly placed individual.

The Legend of Hell House (1973)

Another horror entry scripted by Richard Matheson from his novel of the same name is a thinly disguised remake of Shirley Jackson's *Haunting of Hill House* and may have been intended as Matheson' take on themes raised in that book. (If anyone out there knows the answer, let us know!) Quite possibly the scariest movie ever made, Roddy McDowall and Pamela Franklin lead us through the morbid history of Hell House ("The Mt. Everest of Haunted Houses!") to its bizarre climax. The fog shrouded real life mansion makes for a perfect setting while moody direction by John Hough and one of the most atmospheric scores ever written for a horror movie by Brian Hodgson and Delia Derbyshire only add to the terror. Avoid watching alone or with the lights out! (Adult content)

Our cast as they first set eyes on Hell House: Gayle Hunnicutt as Ann Barret, Roddy McDowall as Benjamin Fischer, Clive Revill as Dr. Lionel Barrett, and Pamela Franklin (all grown up since her role in *The Innocents*) as Florence Tanner.

Pamela Franklin as psychic Florence Tanner is harassed by the spirits haunting *Hell House*.

Also not unaffected is Gayle Hunnicutt as Ann Barrett. When the spirits of autoeroticism strike, she turns seductress trying to lure Roddy McDowall's Ben Fischer into sin…

The secret at the heart of *Hell House:* Michael Gough as Emeric Belasco, who tried to compensate for an affront to his ego by corrupting everyone around him.

The Night Strangler (1973)

Television sequel to the *Night Stalker* of the year before is directed by Dan Curtis and again scripted by Richard Matheson who manages to turn in a story that holds the viewer's interest while keeping within the established plot pattern set by its successful forebear. Darren McGavin reprises his role as reporter Carl Kolchak and Simon Oakland that of his long suffering editor, Tony Vincenzo. This time, the action has moved from the bright lights of Las Vegas to the underground "city" beneath Seattle, Washington where another long lived monster kills beautiful young women for their blood. Despite the similarity in its plot with that of *Stalker*, *Strangler* remains compelling as Kolchak once again pursues clues wherever they lead, dodging official sanction in the form of police and publisher along the way. The film must have been well received because Kolchak's next assignment was his very own weekly TV series!

View of the underground city set, complete with nineteenth century buggies, where the villainous Dr. Malcolm Richards holes up.

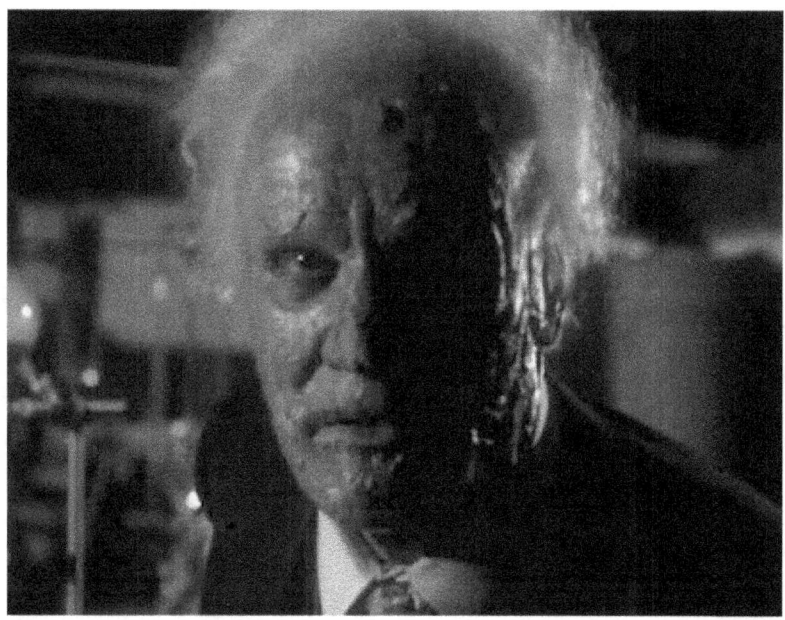

Richard Anderson as Dr. Richard Malcolm or Dr. Malcolm Richards, whichever you prefer. Here, we see what happens when he doesn't take his regular dose of virgin's blood!

For *The Night Strangler*, **the lovely Jo Ann Pflug replaced Carol Lynley as Gail Foster Kolchak's feminine sidekick. Likely, Lynley discovered she had no patience for a boyfriend who couldn't hold down a steady job!**

Move over Stephen King! The real king of horror was Richard Matheson. Besides being the author of many classic short stories and novels (that were adapted to film), Matheson was also a chief writer on the *Twilight Zone* **and scripted a score of classic horror films.**

Phase IV (1974)

An odd film, made the stranger by Saul Bass' quiet direction coupled with impressive and unsettling close up photography of real ants by Ken Middleham. Produced just as *Star Wars* was about to land in theaters like a laser guided bomb, this quiet, even enigmatic film was destined to be one of the last of the old time concept driven SF movies as colonies of desert ants develop intelligence that seems to exceed mankind's own. In an isolated lab, two scientists seek to study the ants but they soon find their positions reversed as they themselves become the object of the ants' scrutiny. Mysteriously, the ants allow an orphaned girl to pass through to the lab and in a final scene that fell victim to the editing room, the girl and younger of the two scientists merge with the collective ant intelligence to become the progenitors of a new ant/human hybrid destined to take over the Earth from mankind! Was it an SF movie or a horror movie? You be the judge!

What did the ants find so interesting about Kendra Eldridge (played by Lynn Frederick)?

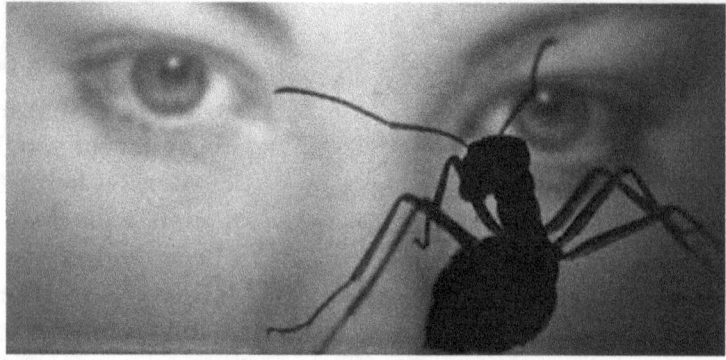

Kendra Eldridge is mesmerized by an ant that has infiltrated the scientist's lab.

At the climax of *Phase IV*, Kendra Eldridge undergoes a strange metamorphosis. Is she destined to be the queen mother of new human/ant hybrids? Who knows? An important montage sequence that would have better explained it all was cut from the end of the movie.

Nigel Davenport as Dr. Ernest Hubbs and Michael Murphy as James Lesko check out strange formations constructed by ants that they've been studying.

The Terminal Man (1974)

Based on the novel of the same name authored by Michael Crichton, *The Terminal Man* is a near future story about an experimental medical procedure involving implanted electrodes to control different functions of the brain. Harry Benson (played by George Segal) is the test subject who suffers from blackouts during which he becomes violent. When he returns to normal, he has no memory of what happened during the blackout. At first, the experiment seems to be successful, but after Benson escapes from the hospital, the implants begin to induce the blackouts more and more frequently until they threaten to become permanent. Meanwhile, doctors and police race to track Benson down before he kills someone…which he does of course. Interestingly directed by Mike Hodges in a quirky, experimental style peculiar to many early 70s films and accompanied by a subdued score that adds to the overall atmosphere of antiseptic strangeness.

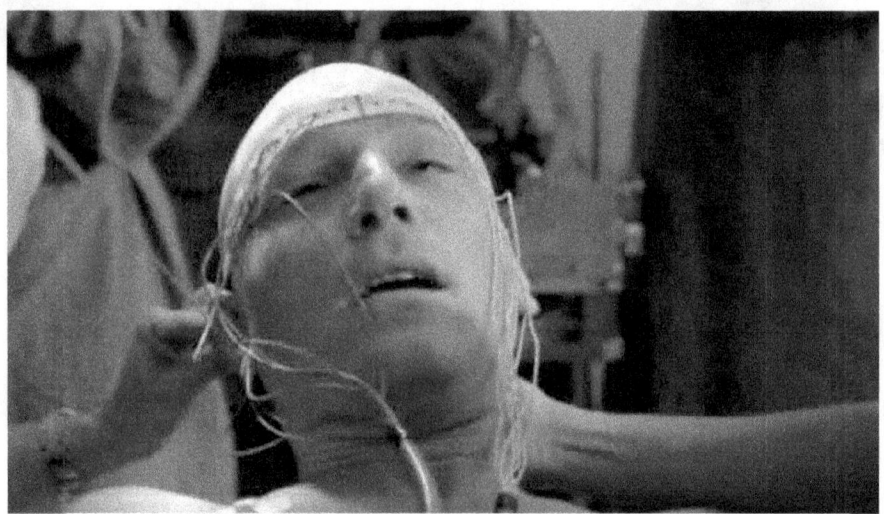

George Segal as Harry Benson is prepped for the operation that will implant computer controlled electrodes in his brain.

Students observe the operation. One of the more interesting aspects of *The Terminal Man* is the detail in which director Mike Hodges goes to depict medical procedures…a hallmark of Crichton's novels.

Joan Hackett as Dr. Janet Ross, is terrorized in her home by a bewigged Harry Benson.

In an earlier scene, Benson kills his girlfriend who helped him escape from the hospital.

Before hitting it really big with novels like *Jurassic Park*, Michael Crichton was a presence on the 70s Hollywood scene with his earliest novels being adapted to film before he himself joined the industry as a director.

The Stepford Wives (1975)

Based on the Ira Levin novel this film is a good example of early 70s directorial sensibilities with oddball shots, lingering takes, and good use of foreshadowing that help accentuate a growing sense of unease as city girl turned suburban housefrau Katherine Ross begins to suspect that things may not be all they appear to be in bucolic Stepford. Good slow burn as clues are laid and friends' personalities are suddenly altered until Ross' character breaks down in a session with her therapist. Although on the face of it a feminist's nightmare, the film is actually a put down of simple minded male chauvinism but a fast paced modern horror yarn for all that. (Adult content)

Katherine Ross plays homemaker and wannabe photographer Joanna Eberhart in *The Stepford Wives*. Here, her suspicions about husband Walter (played by Peter Masterson) seem to be confirmed. In Stepford, you see, things are just too perfect. Real women could never be happy with home and family would they? Of course not!

Katherine Ross as Joanna Eberhart tries to convince the other ladies of Stepford to start thinking more along liberated lines…to no avail.

Oh, the horror! Katherine Ross as Joanna Eberhart before…

…and after her transformation from liberated woman to happy homemaker.

Rollerball (1975)

If you can get past the notion that the cheesy sport of roller derby popular on Saturday afternoon TV in the 70s can be transformed into an exciting futuristic game of violence and death, then you might like *Rollerball*. The movie is set in a near future when the world is governed by a handful of giant corporations (think Apple, Google, Amazon, or Facebook) that keeps the unthinking masses happy with bread and circuses. In this case, the deadly sport of rollerball. The only problem is that Jonathan E (James Caan), its most successful player, has achieved such hero status that he threatens the rule of the corporations. To solve the problem, the powers that be contrive to make the rollerball championship game a no holds barred affair with the hopes that Jonathan E will meet his end. Directed by Norman Jewison and based on a novel by script writer William Harrison, the film moves fairly quickly with the action on the rollerball court fun. Overall, however, the movie's 70s directorial flourishes robs the film of forward momentum and Caan's portrayal of Jonathan E. leaves much to be desired as the would be revolutionary. He is, however, given a nice speech about personal freedom being more valuable than government provided material wealth and easy living…a sentiment that's grown more timely as the 21st century wears on. That said, *Rollerball* remains a relic of an era soon to be swept away by a revolution of another kind: the coming of *Star Wars*.

The rules were changed for the championship rollerball game. Here James Caan as Jonathan E. faces down a motorcycle riding opposition player.

Jonathan E. pauses for breath in the final moments of the championship game.

Like many SF movies of the early 70s, *Rollerball*, taking place as it does in the near future, used existing modernesque structures as locations. Here we have the BMW Building in Munich, Germany.

John Houseman as Mr. Bartholomew hobnobs with the elite who secretly control the world of rollerball.

Maude Adams as Ella is assigned by the corporations to pacify Jonathan E. and convince him to stick with sports.

Trilogy of Terror (1975)

Richard Matheson strikes again with yet more adaptations of his classic stories by himself as scriptwriter as well as friend and fellow fantasy author, William F. Nolan. Another TV movie in the manner of *Night Stalker* and *Night Strangler*, this film is different in that it's comprised of three weird tales with the last one achieving true pop cultural notoriety as actress Karen Black is chased around her modern high rise apartment by a small African fetish doll come to life and bent on killing her. In fact, Black stars in all three tales beginning with "Julie" about a mousy school teacher who's anything but. In the second story, "Millicent and Therese," Black plays a dual role: prudish Millicent and sexy Therese. The final story, called "Amelia" is actually based on Matheson's short story "Prey." Direction by Dan Curtis is functional until he cuts loose on "Prey." Unfortunately, 70s television production values calling for over lit sets makes most of the film seem flat and un-atmospheric. But Matheson and Nolan's scripts are strong enough to overcome that handicap.

In the shocking climax to "Prey," audiences discover that the fetish has won and its evil spirit now inhabits the luckless Amelia (played by Karen Black)!

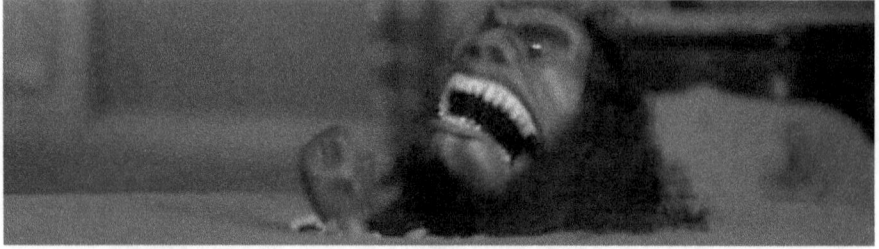

The African fetish rips out of a cardboard box eager to hunt and kill. Would "Prey" even be considered for production in these PC times? Not likely!

Karen Black as the sexy Therese in "Millicent and Therese"

Young men beware! Karen Black entices male students as the secret seductress of "Julia."

The Land that Time Forgot (1975), The People that Time Forgot (1977), and At the Earth's Core (1976)

American International Pictures struck a deal with Edgar Rice Burroughs Inc to produce three films based on some of the author's classic novels beginning with *The Land that Time Forgot*. Although producers eschewed the use of stop motion for the creature FX, overall production values weren't bad. Unfortunately, the route they did choose, use of puppets controlled by rods from underneath designed by Derek Meddings were fun in their clumsy way (use of matte shots and rear screen projection helped) but nowhere near as satisfying as stop motion. The whole thing didn't end up mattering much anyway as an earthquake in the form of *Star Wars* would wipe this kind of old fashioned filmmaking off the map turning these ERB films instantly into quaint holdovers. They did have a couple things going for them though including fairly good adaptations of the original novels, Doug McClure and Patrick Wayne as American imports for the leads and adorable Susan Penhaligon in *Land*, Sarah Douglas in *People*, and Caroline Munro in *Core*. That said, these films are still fun to watch if only as museum pieces for hands on FX without the aid of CGI.

Overall creature FX weren't that bad in the ERB movies. Use of rear screen combined with undercranked miniatures were somewhat effective. Modern audiences approaching them in the wrong frame of mind and watching them today in the advent of ultra realistic CGI may still find them hard to take though.

No CGI was needed for Susan Penhaglion who co-starred in *Land* as biologist Lisa Clayton.

Nor for Sarah Douglas who graced *People* as photographer Charly

The evil Mahars who rule Pellucidar, the world at the Earth's core!

Logan's Run (1976)

Another film made in the same period as *Soylent Green* offers what could have been a sequel to that movie, albeit centuries in the future. Like *Soylent Green*, this film is an adaptation by scripter George Clayton Johnson that is actually superior to its source material, a novel by William F. Nolan. The plot involves a dystopian future where humanity, sequestered in domed cities for centuries and long since having forgotten the existence of the outside world, allow their lives to be controlled by a computer programmed to kill all those inmates who reach the age of 30 through ritualized murder called "carousel." The story follows an enforcer of the computer's edicts (Michael York) and his female friend (Jenny Agutter), as they escape the city to the outside world. SF concepts here are in abundance: ritualized murder, in vitro fertilization, identities reduced to numbers, controlled population growth, plastic surgery for everyone, sex without morality or consequences, and what we would call today, internet sex with selected partners arriving at one's home via matter transporter! The transporter, by the way, is used to good effect when York activates it and receives Agutter draped in one of the most alluring outfits in all SF cinema! The most expensive science fiction film ever until that time, *Logan's Run* has the distinction of being the last traditional SF entry of the 1950-1970s period before it all came to an end with the arrival of *Star Wars* in 1977. It marked the end of an era that began in 1951 with *Day the Earth Stood Still* when ideas were the chief product of SF movies and FX were real, hands on work created by professional craftsmen. From this point on, action seasoned with political correctness and increasing use of Computer Generated Imagery (CGI) would dominate, impoverishing SF cinema, reducing its level of realism, and giving special effects a dull sameness to every effort. And so, *Logan's Run* has proven to be a fitting finale to the classic era of cinematic science fiction as it continues to be one of the best pure sci fi films ever made ending with Logan 5 and Jessica 6 rediscovering the human values of the past, an element needed to give meaning to the often fantastic events in such movies, an element sorely lacking in most subsequent SF films. (Adult content)

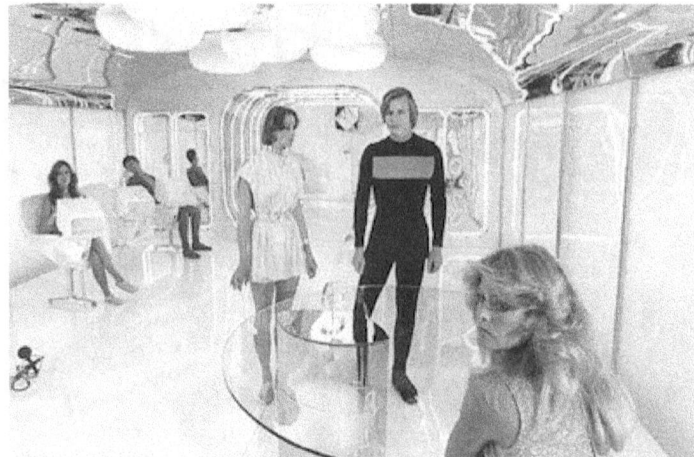

Jessica 6 and Logan 5 arrive at the New You shop to have Logan's face changed enabling him to escape Last Day and seek Sanctuary. *Logan's Run* was chock full of Sci Fi concepts and this instant plastic surgery clinic was a good extrapolation of today's fixation with such procedures.

Move over slave girl Leia! Beautiful Jenny Agutter as Jessica 6 made her debut in *Logan's Run* wearing this spectacular ensemble and SF wardrobes would never be the same again!

Last Day: 30 year olds prepare for suicide disguised as religious ritual. Another concept explored in *Logan's Run* that continues to move toward reality in our own world as politicians legalize euthanasia under ever widening circumstances. Brrr!

Star Wars (1977), The Empire Strikes Back (1980), The Return of the Jedi (1983)

Fast paced, exciting, and admittedly influential, but with the absence of ideas, cliched plots, and bad acting, these films offer little to the connoisseur of the fantastic unless one seeks mindless entertainment. The roller coaster ride begins in *Star Wars* (later subtitled "A New Hope"), continues through *Empire Strikes Back*, and doesn't stop until *Return of the Jedi*. Throughout, producer George Lucas (he directed only the first film) takes his cue from the Saturday afternoon matinees of the 1940s when furiously paced, multi part serials ended in cliff hanger situations. Along the way, audiences are treated to ersatz philosophy, cuddly creatures, and evil bad guys climaxing in a third film that more or less rehashes elements of the first. If there are any complaints to be made about modern SF cinema, one needs go no farther than here. The first "blockbuster" in film history, Hollywood took the wrong lessons from *Star Wars*, with later films concentrating on action over concepts. Ray gun fights and spaceship battle action became the norm as studios realized that there were profits to be made with SF. Audiences had grown younger over the years and were more ready than their elders to accept pure fantasy at the cinema. Consequently, sci fi was taken off the back burner and given A list budgets. More money than ever would be spent on increasingly expensive projects but to little avail. There has been precious little comfort for science fiction purists over the decades since the debut of *Star Wars* with most SF films emulating its worst features.

The new icons: Harrison Ford as Han Solo, Carrie Fisher as Princess Leia, and Mark Hamill as Luke Skywalker. Their characterizations were shallow and cliched but they were enough to strike deep chords of memory in their mostly youthful audiences such that *Star Wars* became the first SF film to achieve blockbuster status.

The climax to *Empire Strikes Back* as we learn, surprise! That the evil lord Darth Vader is actually hero Luke Skywalker's father. Despite the predictability of such plot contrivances, it was the special effects that were the real stars of the *Star Wars* films with sets, vehicles, and their near seamless integration into the action setting a new standard for SF filmmaking.

As the films progressed, so did the level of special effects. Unfortunately, while the FX department constantly improved, the scripts could not keep up. In *Return of the Jedi*, audiences also saw the return of the death star as well as a repeat of the action from the first film as the rebel fleet attempts to destroy it.

Invasion of the Body Snatchers (1978)

A rare instance in which a remake might be as good as the original. Somewhat of a sequel signaled by the appearance of Dr. Miles Bennell (played by Kevin McCarthy reprising his role from the original) at the start of the movie ("They're here! They're here!") the rest of the film pretty much follows the same plot as the first. This time however, the protagonist isn't a medical doctor but San Francisco health inspector Matthew Bennell (played by Donald Sutherland) who becomes involved with the invasion after owners of a local spa insist (as did King Donovan and Carolyn Jones in the original) that something was not right at their place of business. Enter psychologist David Kibner (played by Leonard Nimoy) who poo poos the notion of lookalike replacements. Of course, he's already been replaced himself and soon, Bennell and girlfriend Elizabeth Driscoll (Brook Adams) are on the run from the entire city's population who have also been turned. Director Philip Kaufman ups the ante from the first movie by setting his version in the big city and does a masterful job of double tracking the suspense: viewers are aware of the mounting threat of alien invasion while the characters aren't. The shock ending is already a classic! (Adult content)

Leonard Nimoy (right) as psychologist Dr. David Kibner soothes the irrational fears of Jeff Goldblum as spa owner Jack Belicec (left) and Donald Sutherland as Matthew Bennell.

Brooke Adams as Elizabeth Driscoll fulfills two functions in the new *Body Snatchers*: she continues SF cinematic tradition of including attractive young ladies as co-stars but also answers the burning question from the original film: When Becky Driscoll was replaced, how did she wind up with the same clothes as the original? Or clothed at all? Here, Adams bravely answers that question by parading around in the last scenes of the film in the all together!

Shh! Don't tell anyone, but this is the shocking final shot in the remake of *Invasion of the Body Snatchers!*

Coma (1978)

The first and best of a slew of medical thrillers that have followed in its wake with physicians Robin Cook/novelist and Michael Crichton/director the perfect combination for giving this film its eerie, antiseptic touch. Excellent cast including attractive Genevieve Bujold as the young doctor no one will believe, slick Richard Widmark as the head of the hospital dealing in murder and body parts, and slow on the up-take Michael Douglas as Bujold's boy friend. A clutch of future stars make up the rest of the hospital staff in this believable story of the near-future (although in a world where euthanasia, abortion, and the killing of defective newborns is fast becoming the norm, one could almost be forgiven for wondering what all the fuss is about). (Adult content)

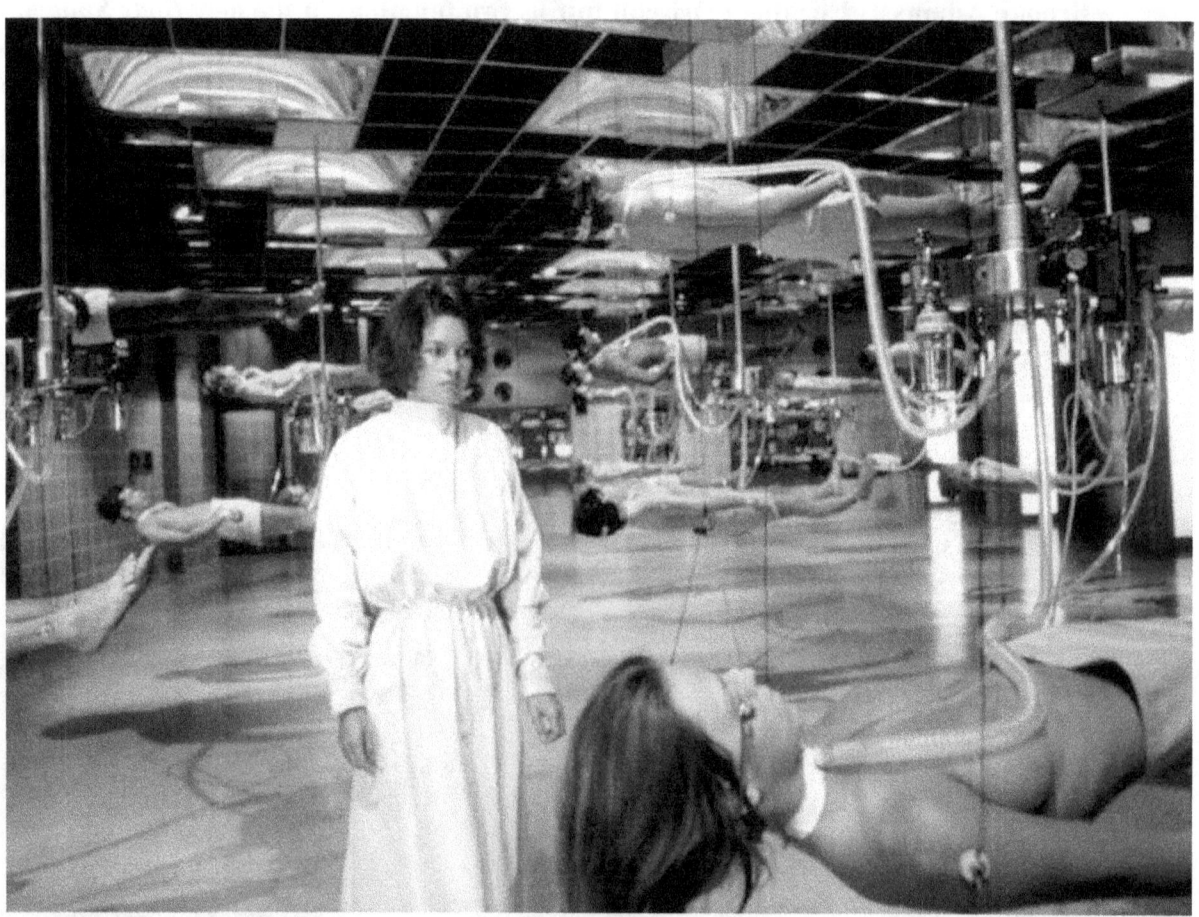

Genevieve Bujold as Dr. Susan Wheeler takes an unauthorized tour of the creepy Jefferson Institute where coma patients are shipped and stored like so much cordwood. In the tradition of pre-*Star Wars* SF films, *Coma* explores ideas and concepts rather FX laden action; something that would become more infrequent as the decades passed.

Cute and perky Genevieve Bujold played Dr. Susan Wheeler, a Nancy Drew clone all grown up.

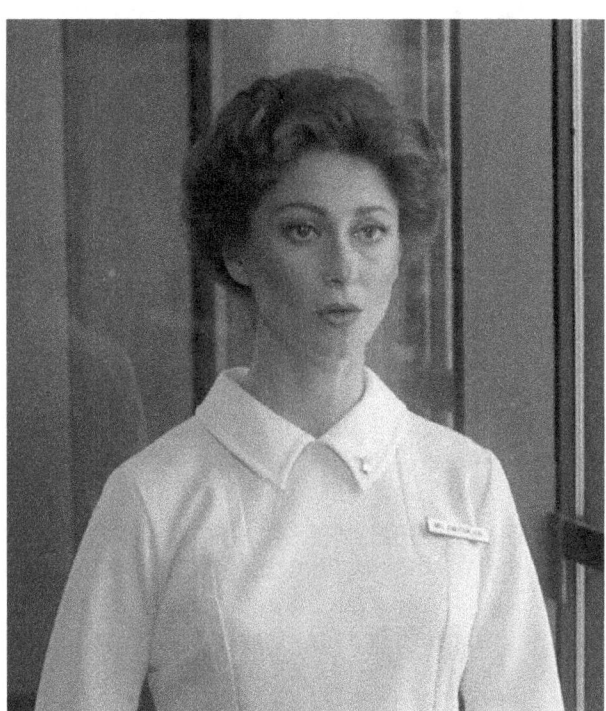

Elizabeth Ashley was perfect as the robotic nurse Emerson, in charge of the Jefferson Institute and who controlled bidding on body parts harvested from its patients. Brrr!

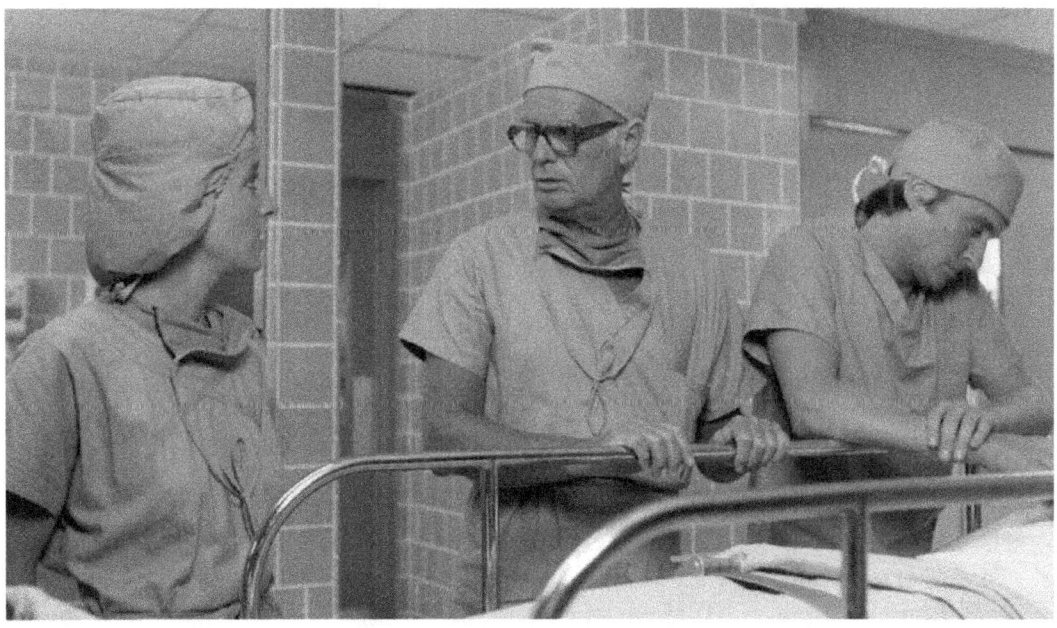

Richard Widmark as the evil Dr. George Harris prepares to perform unnecessary surgery on our heroine! In the style of *Terminal Man*, the hospital atmosphere created in *Coma* is believable with operating room chatter between doctors and nurses while patient is unconscious striking one as realistic.

Star Trek: The Motion Picture (1979), Wrath of Khan (1982), Search for Spock (1984), The Voyage Home (1986), The Final Frontier (1989), The Undiscovered Country (1991)

Somewhat hit or miss and when these films hit, they're less SF than action/adventure/melodrama. The only ones you need to worry about are those based on the classic series (Kirk, Spock, McCoy, etc) and of those only *Star Trek: The Motion Picture, The Wrath of Khan, The Search for Spock*, and *The Undiscovered Country* are worth anyone's while. More appealing as sci fi than the *Star Wars* features, whatever success the *Trek* movies have is largely based on the strength of the characterizations established on the original TV show. Unable to keep up with technical advances of the *Star Wars* films, the level of FX in the *Trek* movies begins strongly with the first installment then dips as the franchise progresses. Still, these are fun, fast moving space adventures with a touch of humor. You've been warned!

Director Robert Wise (left) and creator Gene Roddenberry (dark coat) join the returning cast of the TV show (William Shatner as Capt. Kirk, Deforest Kelly as Dr. McCoy, and Leonard Nimoy as Mr. Spock) on the set of *Star Trek: The Motion Picture*. Unfairly maligned for its slow pace, the film actually captures some of the wonder of space exploration…before morphing into a soft reboot combining elements of earlier TV episodes.

"He tasks me!" Ricardo Montalban hams it up as he reprises his role as Khan from the TV show. *Wrath of Khan* was the best of the all the *Trek* films bar none.

In the dramatic climax to *Search for Spock*, Kirk faces off with the Klingon commander.

Cool ship to ship action that the best of the *Trek* movies did better than anyone else! Here, in *Undiscovered Country*, the Enterprise and Excelsior have a Klingon warship trapped between them.

Alien (1979)

"In space, no one can hear you scream!" At least that's what director Ridley Scott and screenwriter Dan O'Bannon promised us in the trailer to this update of the old haunted house theme. This time, the action takes place in outer space on the good ship Nostromo which leaves its assigned course to investigate a distress signal. The crew finds the source as well as the gestation pods of some kind of alien creature, one of which attaches itself to the face of a hapless crew member. That sets up the film's most memorable scene in which the baby creature bursts from the chest of the crewmember, disappears into the bowels of the ship, and then reappears full grown and hungry! If the rest of the plot sounds familiar, it is. Obviously based on the classic 50s film *It! The Thing From Beyond Space* (which in turn was based on the A.E. van Vogt story "Black Destroyer"), as well as *Planet of the Vampires* the film at least, steals from the best sources. FX and sets are top notch with design work by artist H.R. Giger of particular note. Anyway, the results are good but flawed. The film is entertaining while establishing some new and unpromising tropes for future SF films including crewmembers that resemble space truckers rather than military men as they would have been in the 50s, liberal use of foul language, and iron maidens whose roles seemed to have been written for men before a last minute substitution. All elements that robbed this film as well as future films that copied them of much needed realism. Later films in the franchise were even worse, doubling down as they did on the worst features of *Alien*. Scott would return to the SF genre many times in the future but never achieved even the modicum of success he does here. Beware all sequels. (Adult content)

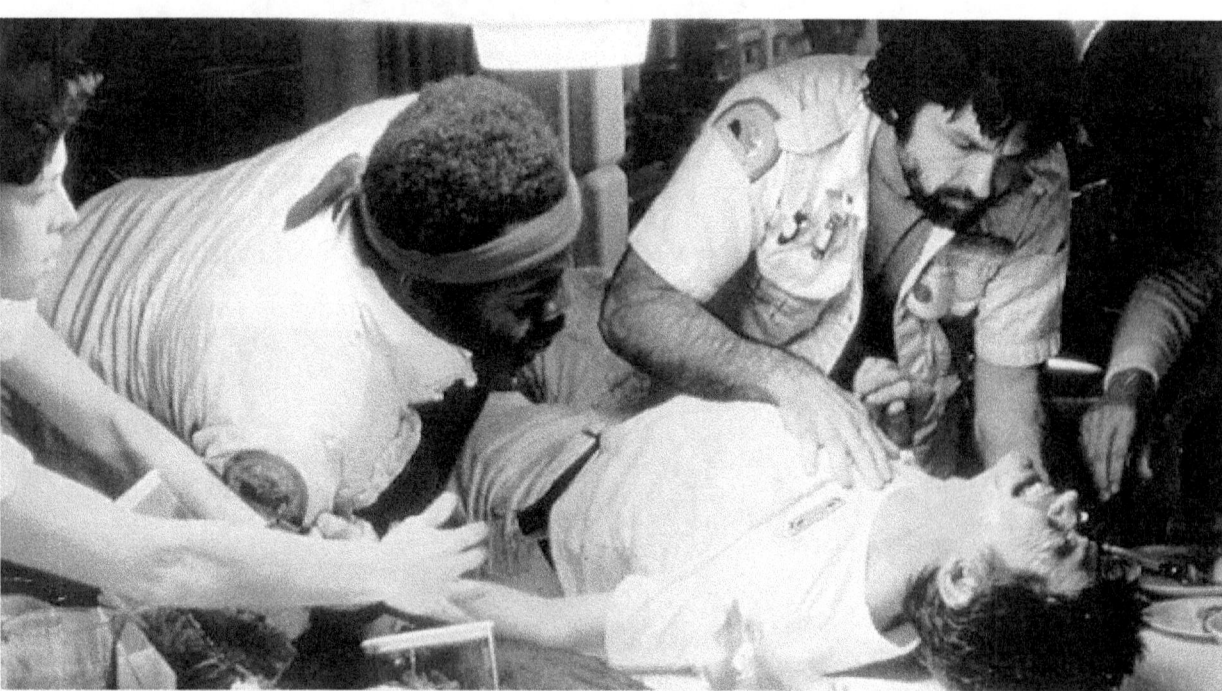

In the film's most harrowing scene, the infant alien bursts from the crewmember's chest in a gory spray. Here, fellow crewmembers display concern as the unfortunate victim convulses on the supper table just before the disturbing event.

Crewmember exploring the wreck of an alien ship discover the remains of its pilot.

The Nostromo on approach to the planet from which a distress signal has been received. The model work as well as interior sets were of *Star Wars* level of articulation and functionality. At last, with studios willing to invest the sums necessary, SF films could create perfectly believable environments within which their otherwise fantastic stories could take place.

Altered States (1980)

Weird but interesting film that skirts the edges of science fiction exploring as it does altered states of consciousness. William Hurt plays Dr. Edward Jessup a psychologist researching the nature of consciousness. To do it, he pursues every crazy avenue including drugs, peyote, and magic mushrooms used by Indians in the southwest. Eventually, he becomes enamored with the use of sensory deprivation techniques that cut off all the senses and theoretically forcing the subconscious to express itself. First experiments revert him to earlier stages of man's evolution until eventually, his mind is taken all the way back to the beginning of creation. Parallel to his experiments however, is his on again off again relationship with girlfriend then wife Emily (played by Blair Brown) who becomes his anchor to reality and ultimately saves him from being literally sucked into a whirlpool representing the chaotic forces that existed before the universe was created. Director Ken Russell tells the story based on a novel by Paddy Chayefsky (who also wrote the script) with often inventive use of FX. Not for the faint hearted but a decent idea driven film on the level of *Andromeda Strain*, *Forbin Project*, and *Terminal Man*. (Adult content)

Strange, symbolic imagery encountered by Dr. Jessup on one of his drug induced visions.

Dr. Jessup as he appears when devolved to a primitive cave man type.

Blair Brown as Emily Jessup, attempts to pull her husband out of the primordial soup from which the universe was created…

An idealized Blair Brown as Emily Jessup is the focus that will be her husband's salvation. Needless adult sequences and blasphemous imagery however, hold back *Altered States* from being fully recommended.

Excalibur (1981)

Faithful and elaborate adaptation of *Le Morte d'Arthur* by writer and director John Boorman captures something of those dark years between the fall of the Roman Empire and the rise of the West when the old ways of faery gave way to the followers of Christ. The film benefits by having been produced in the wake of *Star Wars* when suddenly Hollywood had plenty of money to throw around on various fantasy projects. As a result, production values on *Excalibur* are some of the highest for a movie about the time when knights were bold etc. Heavy looking armor coupled with gasping, groaning battlers fighting with heavy broadswords really conveys a feeling that both sword and armor were as heavy as the real things likely were. Story moves along quickly while capturing a weird, otherworldly atmosphere. Attempt at occasional humor involving Merlin, however, falls flat. (Adult content)

The final battle sequence in *Excalibur* with blood smeared knights fighting under a huge, red sun is one of the most striking images in a film filled with striking images.

Trouble in Camelot: Cherie Lunghi as Guenevere and Nigel Terry as Arthur on their wedding day.

The fabled sword in the stone. In an effort to remain faithful to his source material, Boorman not only recreated key scenes such as Arthur pulling Excalibur from the stone but also the rape of his mother Igrayne by Uther Pendragon. One of the few instances in filmdom where an argument could be made that such a scene was called for.

Helen Mirren as Morgana le Fay anoints her son, Mordred, played by Robert Addie, before sending him out to kill his father, King Arthur.

Outland (1981)

Solid update of classic western, *High Noon,* with a plot that's actually about something and not just an excuse for mindless action as so many post-Star Wars SF films are. Well rounded characters and good FX make this a solid entry with Sean Connery as Marshal William O'Neil standing alone against a gang of drug dealers at a mining colony on Io. Written and directed by Peter Hyams, FX are solid in this post Star Wars, pre-CGI film with interior sets and exterior model work the most impressive. (Adult content)

In his lonely fight against the drug cartel, Sean Connery as Marshal O'Neil, keeps tabs on the bad guys via security cameras around the station.

Peter Boyle plays the conniving mining manager Mark Sheppard. Here, he "suggests" that O'Neil leave his crewmen alone when they decide to "let off steam" when off duty. In reality, he's involved in a scheme to sell illegal drugs to the workers. The cartel makes a profit on the sale and increased energy in the workers helps to meet production schedules.

Frances Sternhagen plays Dr. Marion Lazarus, a washed up MD and the only person in the colony willing to help O'Neil when a group of cartel hitmen arrive to kill him.

Elaborate interior set design was becoming a hall mark of Sf films in the 80s. Here's the living quarters for miners in *Outland*.

O'Neil and his deputy interrogate a prisoner held in a zero g cell!

Blade Runner (1982)

Liberal adaptation of Philip K. Dick's novel, *Do Androids Dream of Electric Sheep?* is stylish, elaborate, even otherworldly, but ultimately dull and pretentious. Script by writers Hampton Fancher and David Peoples is turgid and often impenetrable (they didn't seem to have an ending for the film in mind) with a lead character who often seems to sleepwalk through the picture. Not helping is director Ridley Scott's vision of a dystopian future where it seems the sun is never seen and it never stops raining. The effect was to capture a film noir feel but overkill ruins any hope of that. Classic SF meme involving androids who feel they're human and seek freedom from lives of ownership and planned obsolescence is solid but little if any sympathy for the creatures is generated by the actors. The result is a slow motion film that could have been better. Maybe they should have stuck to the original story? (Adult content)

Seeking freedom and extension of their lives, Darryl Hannah as Pris Stratton and Rutger Hauer as Roy Batty do nothing in appearance and behavior to generate sympathy from the viewer.

Nor does Sean Young as Rachael, the is she or isn't she emotionless android doll that our hero falls for…who knows why!

![Harrison Ford as Rick Deckard]

Harrison Ford is our noir hero sleepwalking through his role as Rick Deckard. His boring, toneless narration available in some versions only adds to the dreariness of his performance.

FX shots such as this harken back to the very beginnings of SF cinema with *Metropolis* and its elaborate cityscapes. Such scenes are by far the best thing about *Bladerunner*.

Something Wicked This Way Comes (1983)

Ray Bradbury's famous novel finally makes it to the big screen in this evocative Disney treatment. Overly dependent on too many FX shots and unfortunate reliance on indoor sets and backlots, the film, as directed by Jack Clayton and scripted in part by Bradbury himself, nevertheless manages to capture a little of what childhood once was. It's only too bad that the film's narration is voiced by actor Arthur Hill rather than Bradbury himself…that would have been the perfect touch! Still, the scene where the boys, listening from their upper story bedrooms, hear the distant sound of an approaching train and dash outside, through a nighted cemetery and end up crouching in the brush as the train carrying the Dark Carnival passes eerily by is pure Bradbury and worth the price of entry!

Jonathan Pryce as Mr. Dark, proprietor of Dark's Pandemonium Carnival was well cast; Jason Robards as Charles Halloway was unfortunate. Robards, never an exciting actor to watch, was the perfect remedy for insomnia.

Almost as stiff and dull as Robards were Shawn Carson as Jim Nightshade and Vidal Peterson as Will Halloway.

Wonderful opening imagery for *Something Wicked* really set a Bradburyesque tone for the film with its autumnal setting and narration by Arthur Hill.

In a typical Bradbury type scene, Vidal Peterson as Will Halloway and Shawn Carson as Jim Nightshade hide out from Mr. Dark among the library shelves. Little do they suspect that he's already found them!

Dune (1984), Frank Herbert's Dune (2000), Children of Dune (2003)

After *Forbidden Planet*, the *Dune* films have included some of the purest SF movies ever made and again, chock full of ideas: warping through space with mind power alone; the spice, melange secreted by giant sand worms control of which means control of a vast, galactic empire; the desert world of Dune/Arrakis and its strange ecology; the off-world boy who becomes Dune's long awaited messiah; the Bene Gesserit sisterhood and its byzantine plot to produce the perfect male through whom they plan to rule the empire. In the first filmed attempt at adapting John Herbert's novel of the same name, production values are surprisingly good for a production company not usually noted for it and the direction of David Lynch (genius or madman? You decide!) is perfect for the story's dark and decadent futurescape. However, a pair of later made for television mini-series were far better. *Frank Herbert's Dune* held closer to the original source material while *Children of Dune* (2003) followed the story into the future adapting the sequels *Children of Dune* and *God Emperor of Dune*. Production values, aided by nascent CGI technology are impressive as well as the musical scores. (Adult content).

Francesca Annis as Lady Jessica and Kyle MacLachlan as Paul Atreides headed a large cast in David Lynch's *Dune*, a film that was often baroque in its characterizations as it was grotesque in imagery.

Saskia Reeves as Lady Jessica in *Frank Herbert's Dune*

Alec Neuman took on the role of the messiah as Paul Atreides in *Frank Herbert's Dune*.

Julie Cox as Princess Irulan, Daniela Amavia as Alia Atreides, and James MacAvoy as Leto II Atreides. *Children of Dune* had the chance to introduce new characters to the Dune cycle. Without the distractions of Lynch's grotesqueries, the TV mini series were able to focus on Herbert's byzantine plot.

2010 (1984)

In an encore performance, writer/director Peter Hyams returns to science fiction with this film. While not as fast moving nor as well cast as *Outland*, *2010* (the sequel to *2001*) does provide decent entertainment while also giving viewers looking for more thoughtful SF some satisfaction. In it, Dr. Heywood Floyd (played by Roy Scheider) conducts the followup voyage to Jupiter to find out what happened to Dave Bowman (Keir Dullea reprises his role from the first film) and discover the reason for the failure of the first mission. After various mishaps (and building international tensions back on Earth), contact with the mysterious monolith is made and a message of peace and goodwill to men is received. The film ends with the suggestion that men will learn to live with one another while the monolith waits on Europa, a moon of Jupiter, for a new race to emerge so that it can again help them in their evolution. Disappointing in its more literal interpretation of the monolith, *2010* also falters in its casting with Scheider lacking charisma, Bob Balaban lacking intelligence as HAL inventor Dr. Chandra, dumb looking John Lithgow as Dr. Walter Curnow, and Helen Mirren as the female Russian ship's captain. Nice to watch for its elaborate sets and model work and pleasant by the numbers plot and characterizations.

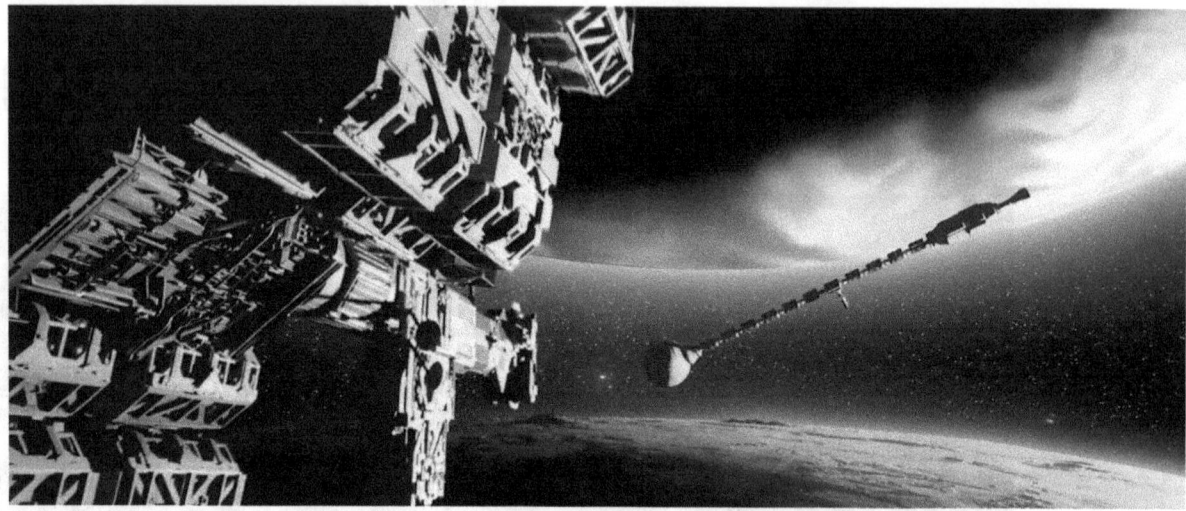

Cool ship to ship FX in *2010*: "The Year We Make Contact!"

Bad casting 1: The viewer is required to believe that the rather not bright looking actor Bob Balaban created the incredibly sophisticated HAL computer system?

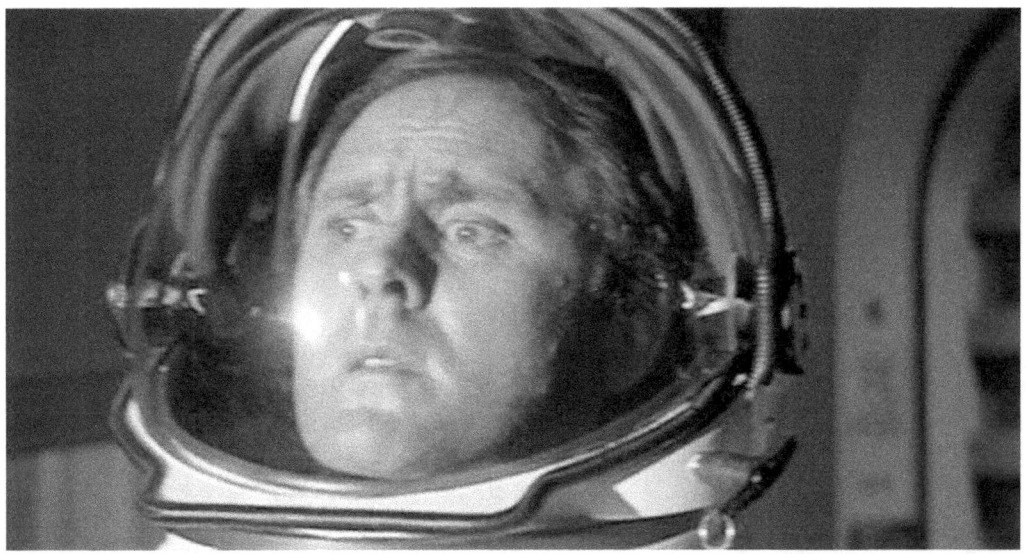

Bad casting 2: The viewer is also asked to believe that John Lithgow with his hang dog looks, is supposed to have been the chief designer of the Discovery, the spaceship from the first movie.

Bad casting 3: Would even the Soviets be foolish enough to trust Helen Mirren to command an important mission costing billions of dollars and that might provide answers to the riddle of the universe?